SIGN REF

(signs used in the maps and diagrams)

Good footpath
(sufficiently distinct to be followed in mist)

Intermittent footpath
(difficult to follow in mist)

Route recommended
    but no path
(if recommended one way only, arrow indicates direction)

Wall ∞∞∞∞∞∞∞∞   Broken wall ∘∘∘∘∘∘∘∘∘∘∘∘∘∘

Fence ++++++++++++   Broken fence ''''''''''''''''''''

Marshy ground ↯↯↯↯↯↯   Trees 🌳🌳🌳🌳🌳🌳

Crags 🪨🪨🪨🪨   Boulders ▵▵▵▵▵▵

Stream or River
        (arrow indicates direction of flow)

Waterfall   Bridge

Buildings ▪▪   Unenclosed road ::::::::::::::::::::::::

Contours (at 100' intervals)   1900
                                     1800
                                     1700

Summit-cairn ▲   Other (prominent) cairns △

A PICTORIAL GUIDE
TO THE
LAKELAND FELLS

SECOND EDITION
REVISED BY CHRIS JESTY

being an illustrated account
of a study and exploration
of the mountains in the
English Lake District

by

AWainwright

BOOK TWO
THE FAR EASTERN FELLS

Frances Lincoln Limited
4 Torriano Mews
Torriano Avenue
London NW5 2RZ
www.franceslincoln.com

First edition published by Henry Marshall, Kentmere, 1957
First published by Frances Lincoln 2003
Second (revised) edition published by Frances Lincoln 2005

Printed and bound in Singapore

A CIP catalogue record is available for this book
from the British Library.

ISBN 0 7112 2466 8

9 8 7 6 5 4 3 2 1

THIS REVISED AND UPDATED EDITION PUBLISHED BY
FRANCES LINCOLN, LONDON

FOREWORD
BY BETTY WAINWRIGHT

FOREWORD

The Pictorial Guides have never before been revised, for the reasons given by AW in his concluding remarks to the third volume, *The Central Fells*, where he wrote that by the time he had finished Book Seven, age would prevent him undertaking the 'joyful task' of revising the series himself. He went on to write:

> ... Substantially, of course, the books will be useful for many years to come, especially in the detail and description of the fell tops, while the views will remain unaltered for ever, assuming that falling satellites and other fancy gadgets of man's invention don't blow God's far worthier creations to bits. But, this dire possibility apart, the books must inevitably show more and more inaccuracies as the years go by. Therefore, because it is unlikely that there will ever be revised editions, and because I should just hate to see my name on anything that could not be relied on, the probability is that the books will progressively be withdrawn from publication after a currency of a few years.

This was written in 1958, when the oldest volume was only three years old and by the time he had completed Book Seven in 1965 he was even more conscious of the little things that had gone out of date in the previous volumes — cairns demolished or built, screes eroded, woods felled or grown up, new paths made. As the years passed and it became apparent that the books were still in demand, despite these inaccuracies, he was occasionally approached by people asking for revised editions. But the core of the problem was that, as old age approached, he knew he could not undertake the changes himself, nor did he trust anyone to do the work as he would have wished.

When, in 1980, Chris Jesty broached the idea to him, he was told 'after my lifetime'. This was half the battle won — AW knew Chris's work well, and did trust him. Now, given the continuing popularity and use of the Pictorial Guides, I am delighted that, due to Chris's commitment, the guides are being revised and I give them my blessing. It is with pleasure that I picture Chris re-walking and checking and, where necessary, correcting every route, every ascent and every path. Although most of the individual corrections are minor, the overall impact is huge, and I feel proud and confident — as I am sure AW would be too — that the revised guides will satisfy the needs of the 21st-century walker.

Betty Wainwright
Kendal, 2005

INTRODUCTION
TO THE
SECOND EDITION
BY CHRIS JESTY

INTRODUCTION TO THE SECOND EDITION

In 1959 I went on an Outward Bound course at Eskdale Green, which involved a lot of walking in the mountains. I found that the depiction of paths on Ordnance Survey maps left definite room for improvement, and I had the idea of producing a guide book that would make it easier for people to find their way around. But in 1961 I was given one of Wainwright's Pictorial Guides to the Lakeland Fells and discovered that he had beaten me to it.

It occurred to me that one day the books would become out of date, and that, as I was presumably much younger than the author, the time might arrive when I would be allowed to revise them. It has taken more than forty years for that dream to turn into a reality.

In the meantime I had made the acquaintance of the author. I collaborated with him on *A Guide to the View from Scafell Pike*, and later on, when his eyesight was failing, I drew the maps for two of his other books (*Wainwright in the Limestone Dales* and *Wainwright's Favourite Lakeland Mountains*). Shortly before he died he requested that if ever the Lakeland Guides were to be revised I should be offered the job.

When, in 2003, following a change of publisher, the proposal was revived, I threw myself into the job with enthusiasm. I had a number of advantages over the author. I had a car, I had satellite navigation equipment, I was able to work on enlargements of the pages, and as I didn't have a job I was able to devote all my time and all my energy to this vast project.

Every feature on the maps and ascent diagrams and every word of text have been checked, but I have not checked every recommended route without a path. Descriptions of natural features and views are virtually unaltered, but the number of changes that have been made to maps and ascent diagrams is enormous. The decision was taken to print the paths in a second colour so that they stand out from other details, and also so that readers can tell at a glance that it is the revised edition they are using.

Summit altitudes have been corrected where they differ by five feet or more from the latest Ordnance Survey figures. Parking information has been added where appropriate. I have also taken the liberty of adding other information that seems to me to be of interest. No changes have been made to drawings of landscapes, natural features or buildings, or, of course, to Wainwright's 'Personal Notes in Conclusion'.

Occasional references will be found in the books to Bartholomew's maps. These are still available, but they are now published by Collins.

In order to keep the books as accurate as possible, and in anticipation of future revised editions, readers are invited to write to me (c/o the publishers) about any errors they find in the revised Pictorial Guides. Emails to chrisj@frances-lincoln.com and letters sent to me c/o Frances Lincoln, 4 Torriano Mews, Torriano Avenue, London NW5 2RZ, will be passed on regularly.

Chris Jesty
Kendal, January 2005

BOOK TWO

is dedicated to
the memory of

THE MEN WHO BUILT THE STONE WALLS,

which have endured
the storms of centuries
and remain to this day as monuments to
enterprise, perseverance and hard work

INTRODUCTION

Classification and Definition

Any division of the Lakeland fells into geographical districts must necessarily be arbitrary, just as the location of the outer boundaries of Lakeland must always be a matter of opinion. Any attempt to define internal or external boundaries is certain to invite criticism, and he who takes it upon himself to say where Lakeland starts and finishes, or, for example, where the Central Fells merge into the Southern Fells and *which* fells *are* the Central Fells and which the Southern and *why* they need be so classified, must not expect his pronouncements to be generally accepted.

Yet for present purposes some plan of classification and definition must be used. County and parochial boundaries are no help, nor is the recently-defined area of the Lakeland National Park, for this book is concerned only with the high ground.

First, the external boundaries.   Straight lines linking the extremities of the outlying lakes enclose all the higher fells very conveniently. There are a few fells of lesser height to the north and east, however, that are typically Lakeland in character and cannot properly be omitted : these are brought in, somewhat untidily, by extending the lines in those areas. Thus:

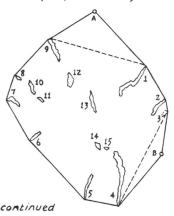

1 : *Ullswater*
2 : *Hawes Water*
3 : proposed *Swindale Resr*
4 : *Windermere*
5 : *Coniston Water*
6 : *Wast Water*
7 : *Ennerdale Water*
8 : *Loweswater*
9 : *Bassenthwaite Lake*
10 : *Crummock Water*
11 : *Buttermere*
12 : *Derwent Water*
13 : *Thirlmere*
14 : *Grasmere*
15 : *Rydal Water*
A : *Caldbeck*
B : *Longsleddale* (church)

continued

Classification and Definition

continued

The complete Guide includes all the fells in the area enclosed by the straight lines of the diagram. This is an undertaking quite beyond the compass of a single volume, and it is necessary, therefore, to divide the area into convenient sections, making the fullest use of natural boundaries (lakes, valleys and low passes) so that each district is, as far as possible, self-contained and independent of the rest.

This division gives seven areas, each with a well-defined group of fells, and each area is the subject of a separate volume

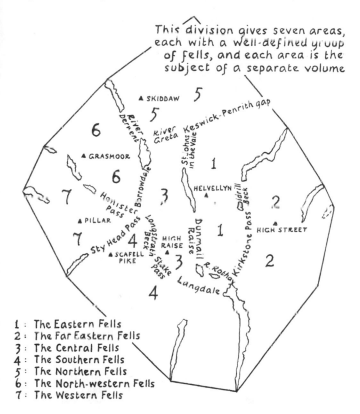

1 : The Eastern Fells
2 : The Far Eastern Fells
3 : The Central Fells
4 : The Southern Fells
5 : The Northern Fells
6 : The North-western Fells
7 : The Western Fells

INTRODUCTION

Notes on the Illustrations

THE MAPS .... Many excellent books have been written
about Lakeland, but the best literature of all for the walker
is that published by the Director General of Ordnance Survey,
the 1" map for companionship and guidance on expeditions, the
2½" map for exploration both on the fells and by the fireside.
These admirable maps are remarkably accurate topographically
but there is a crying need for a revision of the paths on the hills:
several walkers' tracks that have come into use during the past
few decades, some of them now broad highways, are not shown at
all; other paths still shown on the maps have fallen into neglect
and can no longer be traced on the ground.

    The popular Bartholomew 1" map is a
beautiful picture, fit for a frame, but this
too is unreliable for paths; indeed here the
defect is much more serious, for routes are
indicated where no paths ever existed, nor
ever could — the cartographer has preferred
to take precipices in his stride rather than
deflect his graceful curves over easy ground.

    Hence the justification for the maps in this book: they have
the one merit (of importance to walkers) of being dependable as
regards delineation of *paths*. They are intended as supplements
to the Ordnance Survey maps, certainly not as substitutes.

THE VIEWS .... Various devices have
been used to illustrate the views from the
summits of the fells. The full panorama
in the form of an outline drawing is most
satisfactory generally, and this method
has been adopted for the main viewpoints.

THE DIAGRAMS OF ASCENTS .... The routes of ascent
of the higher fells are depicted by diagrams that do not pretend
to strict accuracy: they are neither plans
nor elevations; in fact there is deliberate
distortion in order to show detail clearly:
usually they are represented as viewed
from imaginary 'space-stations.' But it is
hoped they will be useful and interesting.

THE DRAWINGS .... The drawings at least are honest attempts
to reproduce what the eye sees: they illustrate features of
interest and also serve the dual purpose of breaking up the
text and balancing the layout of the pages, and of filling up
awkward blank spaces, like this:

Thirlmere

THE
FAR EASTERN
FELLS

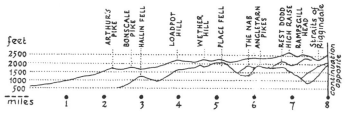

The Far Eastern Fells rise to the east of Kirkstone Pass and the Patterdale valley, which together form a natural western boundary to the group. To north and south these fells run down to low country, and it is on the east side that difficulty arises in fixing a demarcation line, for here high ground continues, to merge ultimately into the Pennines. Nevertheless, it is possible to adopt a satisfactory boundary, not so much by a selection of obvious natural features as by observation of the characteristics of the fells in this area. Lakeland's fells have a charm that is unique: they are romantic in atmosphere, dramatic in appearance, colourful, craggy, with swift-running sparkling streams and tumbled lichened boulders— and the walker along this eastern fringe constantly finds himself passing from the exciting beauty that is typically Lakeland to the quieter and more sombre attractiveness that is typically Pennine. Broadly, this 'æsthetic' boundary runs along the eastern watersheds of Longsleddale, Mosedale and Swindale.

The group has a main spine running through it, due north and south, that keeps consistently above 2000' over a distance of eight miles and culminates midway in the greatest of these fells, High Street. From this central point there is a general decline in altitude

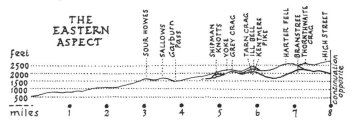

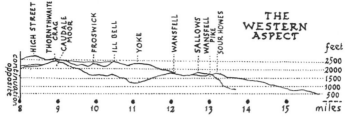

towards the boundaries of the group in all directions
but it is not to be inferred that all ridges radiate
from High Street: on the contrary, it is the pivot of
a complicated system of parallel and lateral ridges
separated by deep valleys that contributes greatly
to the attractiveness of these fells east of Kirkstone
    The relative inaccessibility of many of the heights
(due to a decided lack of tourist accommodation in
the valleys) can be the only reason why they remain
lonely and unfrequented by visitors, for in the high
quality of the scenery and the excellence of the walks
they rank with the best. In one respect, indeed, they
are supreme, for their extensive and uplifting views
across to the distant Pennines are a delight not to
be found elsewhere in the district. Solitary walkers
will enjoy the area immensely, but they must tread
circumspectly and avoid accident. Mountain-camps
and bivouacs offer the best means of exploration; for
the walker who prefers a bed, Mardale Head used to
be the best centre but now has no hospitality nearer
than the Haweswater Hotel (which is badly sited for
travellers on foot) and the Patterdale valley is most
convenient as a base. The area will be appreciated
best, however, if occasional nights can be arranged
at Howtown, Haweswater, Kentmere and Troutbeck.

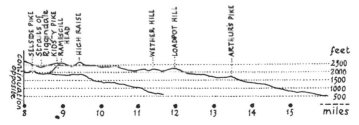

THE FAR EASTERN FELLS

Natural Boundaries

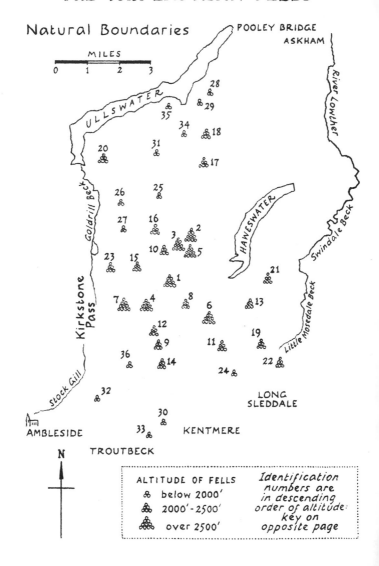

POOLEY BRIDGE
ASKHAM

River Lowther

MILES
0 1 2 3

ULLSWATER

Goldrill Beck

HAWESWATER

Swindale Beck

Little Mosedale Beck

Kirkstone Pass

Stock Gill

AMBLESIDE

TROUTBECK

KENTMERE

LONG SLEDDALE

N

ALTITUDE OF FELLS
  below 2000'
  2000'-2500'
  over 2500'

Identification numbers are in descending order of altitude: key on opposite page

THE FAR EASTERN FELLS

in the order of their appearance in this book

Reference to map opposite: over 2500'	2000'-2500'	below 2000'		Altitude in feet
		26	ANGLETARN PIKES	1857
		28	ARTHUR'S PIKE	1747
		31	BEDA FELL	1670
		29	BONSCALE PIKE	1718
	13		BRANSTREE	2339
		27	BROCK CRAGS	1842
7			CAUDALE MOOR	2502
	12		FROSWICK	2359
	15		GRAY CRAG	2286
	22		GREY CRAG	2093
		35	HALLIN FELL	1271
6			HARTER FELL	2552
	23		HARTSOP DODD	2028
2			HIGH RAISE	2634
1			HIGH STREET	2718
	9		ILL BELL	2484
	11		KENTMERE PIKE	2397
5			KIDSTY PIKE	2560
	10		THE KNOTT	2423
	18		LOADPOT HILL	2201
	8		MARDALE ILL BELL	2496
		25	THE NAB	1887
	20		PLACE FELL	2154
3			RAMPSGILL HEAD	2598
	16		REST DODD	2283
		30	SALLOWS	1691
	21		SELSIDE PIKE	2149
		24	SHIPMAN KNOTTS	1926
		33	SOUR HOWES	1585
		34	STEEL KNOTTS	1414
	19		TARN CRAG	2176
4			THORNTHWAITE CRAG	2569
		36	TROUTBECK TONGUE	1191
		32	WANSFELL	1597
	17		WETHER HILL	2210
	14		YOKE	2316
7	16	13		
	36			

Each fell is the subject of a separate chapter

Howtown •

▲ PLACE FELL
• Patterdale
  ▲ ANGLETARN
    PIKES

• Hartsop

HIGH STREET ▲

MILES
0   1   2   3   4

from Brothers Water

NATURAL FEATURES

The distinctive double summit of Angletarn Pikes is a familiar feature high above the Patterdale valley: the two sharp peaks arrest attention from a distance and are no less imposing on close acquaintance, being attainable only by rock-scrambling, easy or difficult according to choice of route. The western flank of the fell drops steeply in slopes of bracken to the pleasant strath of the Goldrill Beck; on this side Dubhow Crag and Fall Crag are prominent. More precipitous is the eastern face overlooking the quiet deer sanctuary of Bannerdale, where the great bastion of Heck Crag is a formidable object rarely seen by walkers. The fell is a part of a broad curving ridge that comes down from the High Street watershed and continues to Boredale Hause, beyond which Place Fell terminates it abruptly.

The crowning glory of the Pikes, however, is the tarn from which they are named, cradled in a hollow just below the summit. Its indented shore and islets are features unusual in mountain tarns, and it has for long, and deservedly, been a special attraction for visitors to Patterdale. The charms of Angle Tarn, at all seasons of the year, are manifold: in scenic values it ranks amongst the best of Lakeland tarns.

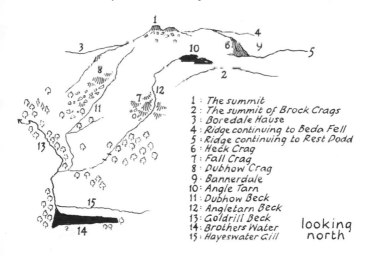

1 : The summit
2 : The summit of Brock Crags
3 : Boredale Hause
4 : Ridge continuing to Beda Fell
5 : Ridge continuing to Rest Dodd
6 : Heck Crag
7 : Fall Crag
8 : Dubhow Crag
9 : Bannerdale
10 : Angle Tarn
11 : Dubhow Beck
12 : Angletarn Beck
13 : Goldrill Beck
14 : Brothers Water
15 : Hayeswater Gill

looking
north

Angletarn Pikes 3

Red Screes and
Brothers Water
from the top of
Dubhow Beck

Heck Crag
from the
Patterdale-
Martindale path

MAP

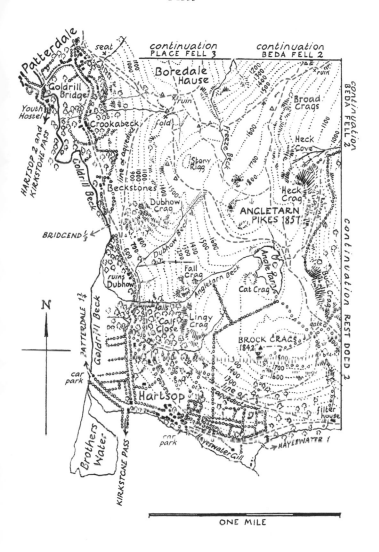

ONE MILE

ASCENT FROM PATTERDALE
1400 feet of ascent : 1¾ miles
Note that this is the initial part of the route to High Street

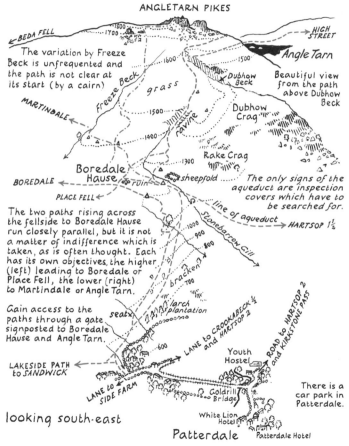

ANGLETARN PIKES

BEDA FELL

HIGH STREET

Angle Tarn

The variation by Freeze Beck is unfrequented and the path is not clear at its start (by a cairn)

Freeze Beck

grass

Dubhow Beck

Beautiful view from the path above Dubhow Beck

MARTINDALE

Dubhow Crag

ravine

Rake Crag

The only signs of the aqueduct are inspection covers which have to be searched for.

Boredale Hause

sheepfold

BOREDALE

ruin

line of aqueduct

HARTSOP 1½

PLACE FELL

Stonebarron Gill

The two paths rising across the fellside to Boredale Hause run closely parallel, but it is not a matter of indifference which is taken, as is often thought. Each has its own objectives, the higher (left) leading to Boredale or Place Fell, the lower (right) to Martindale or Angle Tarn.

bracken

Gain access to the paths through a gate signposted to Boredale Hause and Angle Tarn.

seat

larch plantation

LANE to CROOKABECK ¼ and HARTSOP 2

Youth Hostel

ROAD to HARTSOP 2 and KIRKSTONE PASS

LAKESIDE PATH to SANDWICK

LANE to SIDE FARM

Goldrill Bridge

There is a car park in Patterdale.

White Lion Hotel

Patterdale

Patterdale Hotel

looking south-east

This delightful walk should be in the itinerary of all who stay at Patterdale; the climb is pleasant and the views excellent. Combined with a detour to Angle Tarn, it is an easy half-day's excursion.

ASCENT FROM MARTINDALE
1300 feet of ascent : 3½ miles from Martindale Old Church

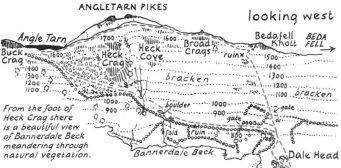

ANGLETARN PIKES

looking west

Angle Tarn — 1700 — Heck Cove — 1600 — Broad Crags — Bedafell Knott — BEDA FELL

Buck Crag — 1600 — Heck Crag — ruin× — 1500 — 1400 — 1300 — 1200 — 1100 — bracken

bracken

1000 — 900 — boulder — gate — gate

From the foot of Heck Crag there is a beautiful view of Bannerdale Beck meandering through natural vegetation.

fold — ruin — 800

Bannerdale Beck

Dale Head

700

Dale Head farmhouse is interesting architecturally

ROAD TO MARTINDALE CHURCH 1½

Two routes are illustrated; both are good.

The valley route, by the wall, is an example of a beautiful and interesting footway falling from favour simply because few now know of it. It ascends the secluded and unfrequented valley of Bannerdale, passes below Heck Crag by a sporting path on steep scree and crosses a low saddle to Angle Tarn, which comes into view suddenly and dramatically: the highlight of the walk. An easy climb (right) leads to the top.

The more direct way makes use of the path to Patterdale, but turns left when the ridge is gained and keeps to the Bannerdale edge until the summit is close on the right.

If the return is to be made to Martindale, use the valley route for the ascent (because of the sudden revelation of Angle Tarn, a surprise worth planning) and the ridge route for descent.

THE SUMMIT

The north (main) summit

Angle Tarn from the south summit

Twin upthrusts of rock, 200 yards apart, give individuality to this unusual summit; the northerly is the higher. Otherwise the top is generally grassy, with an extensive peat bog in a depression.

DESCENTS : Routes of ascent may be reversed. (Note that, to find the Bannerdale valley-path, it is necessary first to descend to Angle Tarn and there cross the low saddle on the left just to the north of a peat gully). In mist, there is comfort in knowing that the path for Patterdale is only 100 yards distant down the west slope.

THE VIEW

Principal Fells

Although the view is largely confined by surrounding heights to a five-mile radius it is full of interest. The abrupt summit gives splendid depth and fall to the prospect south-west, where there is a beautiful picture of Brothers Water and Kirkstonefoot. Deepdale, directly below, is especially well seen.

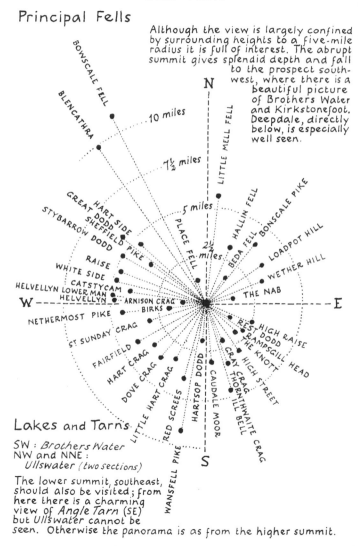

Lakes and Tarns

SW : *Brothers Water*
NW and NNE :
    Ullswater (two sections)

The lower summit, southeast, should also be visited; from there is a charming view of *Angle Tarn* (SE) but *Ullswater* cannot be seen. Otherwise the panorama is as from the higher summit.

RIDGE ROUTES

To BEDA FELL, 1670' : 2 miles
NE, then N and NE   *300 feet*
Main depression at 1450'   *of ascent*
and several minor depressions
An easy walk, the latter part being dull.
Aim for the high knoll north-east, where
an interesting path leads down a
narrowing shoulder (good views of
Bannerdale and Heck Crag here).
The Patterdale-Martindale path
is crossed as it tops the ridge.
   Beyond, the walk becomes
uninteresting. *Beda Fell is
dangerous in mist, having
precipitous crags on the
eastern flank, and the
ridge is ill-defined
beyond the summit.*

The
Patterdale-
Martindale
path is an easy
way of escape
in bad weather;
there is a cairn
at the cross-paths.

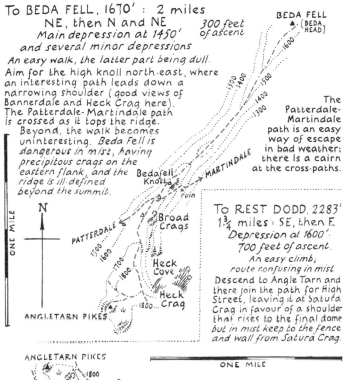

To REST DODD, 2283'
1¾ miles : SE, then E
Depression at 1600'.
700 feet of ascent.
An easy climb;
route confusing in mist
Descend to Angle Tarn and
there join the path for High
Street, leaving it at Satura
Crag in favour of a shoulder
that rises to the final dome
but in mist keep to the fence
and wall from Satura Crag.

ONE MILE

From the cairn on Satura Crag
(only 25 yards from the path)
there is a splendid view of
Bannerdale, a view often
missed by walkers
along this route.

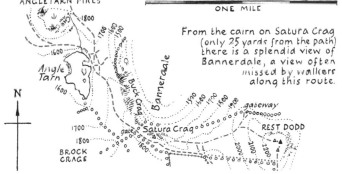

Arthur's Pike

1747'

- Pooley Bridge
  - Askham

▲ ARTHUR'S PIKE

- Howtown

▲ LOADPOT HILL

MILES
0   1   2   3   4

from the Howtown road

NATURAL FEATURES

Arthur's Pike is the northerly termination of the long High Street range, and, like the northerly termination of the parallel Helvellyn range, it contrasts with the usual Lakeland fell-structure by exhibiting its crags to the afternoon sun; the northern and eastern slopes, which are commonly roughest, are without rock. The steep flank falling to Ullswater has several faces of crag below the summit-rim, and, especially around the vicinity of Swarthbeck Gill, which forms the southern boundary of the fell, acres of tumbled boulders testify to the roughness of the impending cliffs and the power of the beck in flood. Above the crags, there is little to excite, and the summit merges without much change in elevation into the broad expanses of Loadpot Hill. The gradual northern slope is partly clothed with heather.

MAP

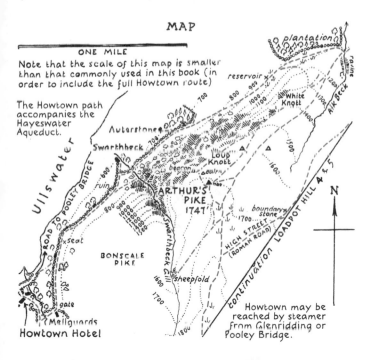

ONE MILE

Note that the scale of this map is smaller than that commonly used in this book (in order to include the full Howtown route)

The Howtown path accompanies the Hayeswater Aqueduct.

Howtown may be reached by steamer from Glenridding or Pooley Bridge.

Ullswater, from the Howtown path

ASCENTS

Arthur's Pike looks particularly forbidding from the Howtown path, by which it is usually climbed, and the timid walker who doubts the wisdom of proceeding will be reassured to discover that the ascent is not only not intimidating but surprisingly easy and everywhere pleasant, *if the route shown on the map is followed.* The obvious and direct alternative by the Swarthbeck ravine is anything but obvious and direct when attempted, and nervous pedestrians should keep away from it.

For the approaches from Askham, Helton and Pooley Bridge, the chapter on Loadpot Hill should be consulted.

THE SUMMIT

Above the edge of the steep Ullswater flank, grassy undulations culminate in a conical knoll crowned by a large cairn; nearby is a short stretch of broken wall. There are no distinct paths on the top, but an indefinite cairned track skirts the precipice, on the brink of which is a well-made beacon; and on the eastern side is a good path that is continuous from Moor Divock to Loadpot Hill. The beacon cannot be seen from the summit-cairn; it stands 250 yards distant in the direction of Blencathra.

THE VIEW

Principal Fells

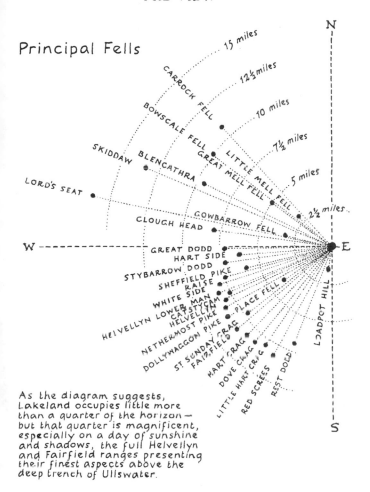

As the diagram suggests, Lakeland occupies little more than a quarter of the horizon — but that quarter is magnificent, especially on a day of sunshine and shadows, the full Helvellyn and Fairfield ranges presenting their finest aspects above the deep trench of Ullswater.

Lakes and Tarns

W to N: Ullswater (two sections: middle and lower reaches)
Ullswater is better seen from the beacon : an impressive sight.

RIDGE ROUTES

To LOADPOT HILL, 2201' : 2¼ miles
S. then SSW, SSE and finally N
Minor depressions : 500 feet of ascent
A dull, easy walk, which is not recommended in mist

Follow the path to the south from the summit. In 200 yards this joins a clearer path going the same way. When the path bears right at Lambert Lad, keep straight on to Loadpot Hill. Alternatively, stay on the main path to the remains of Lowther House, where turn north to the summit-cairn and Ordnance Survey column. *This is not a walk for a wet day, and the whole of this moorland is a nightmare in mist.*

To BONSCALE PIKE, 1718'
1 mile : S. then SSW and NW
Depression at 1575'
150 feet of ascent
A simple walk which should not be attempted in mist.

Follow the path to the south from the summit and bear right to a sheepfold in the depression between the two Pikes. Cross the beck and slant over grassy slopes to the right. *Swarthbeck Gill is dangerous below the fold.*

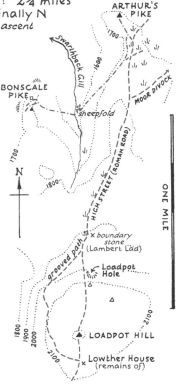

Ullswater, from the beacon

Swarthbeck Gill

Swarthbeck Gill, if it were but more accessible, would be one of the showplaces of the district. Here, between towering rockwalls, are beautiful cataracts, but, alas, they are out of the reach of the average explorer. The ferny, tree-clad lower gorge, however, may (and should) be visited. The prudent venture no further!

Beda Fell

1670'

summit named Beda Head

from Hallin Fell

Beda Fell is the long north-east ridge of Angletarn Pikes, narrowing as it descends; but midway it asserts itself, broadens considerably and rises to a definite summit, Beda Head, which is the geographical centre of the quiet, enchanting, exquisitely beautiful area known affectionately as "Martind'l." Beyond this top the descent continues over the rocky spine of Winter Crag to valley-level at Sandwick on Ullswater. The fell, although mainly grassy, with bracken, has a most impressive east face, broken into three great tiers of crag. It is bounded by deep valleys, Boredale, Bannerdale and Howe Grain, whose combined waters meet at its northern tip.

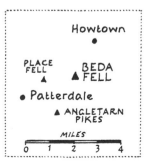

MAP

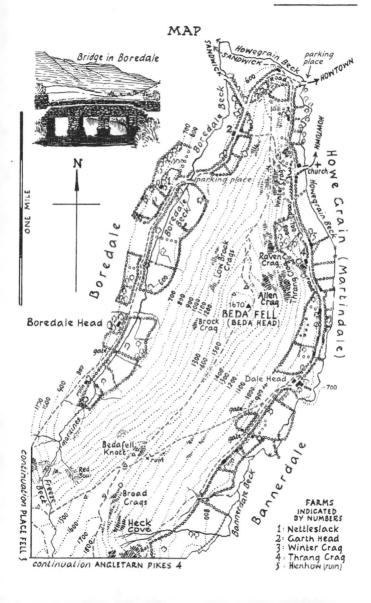

Bridge in Boredale

ONE MILE

N

continuation PLACE FELL 3

continuation ANGLETARN PIKES 4

Howegrain Beck

parking place

HOWTOWN

SANDWICK

Boredale Beck

600

Road

HOWTOWN

church

Howe Grain (Martindale)

Howegrain Beck

700

2 Garth Head

700

600

parking place

Boredale Beck

3 Winter Crag

Boredale

Boredale Head

600

600

700

800

900

1000

1100

Low Brock Crags

Raven Crag

Allen Crag

1670'

BEDA FELL (BEDA HEAD)

Brock Crag

1300

1400

1500

Thrang Crag

4

Dale Head

1200

1100

1000

700

gate

gate

Bannerdale Beck

Bannerdale

1700

1000

900

800

ruin

gate

1300

1200

Freeze Beck

Bedafell Knott

Red Scar

ruin

Broad Crags

800

Heck Cove

1500

1600

1700

FARMS
INDICATED
BY NUMBERS

1: Nettleslack
2: Garth Head
3: Winter Crag
4: Thrang Crag
5: Henhow (ruin)

ASCENTS FROM MARTINDALE AND BOREDALE
1100 feet of ascent : 1¾ miles

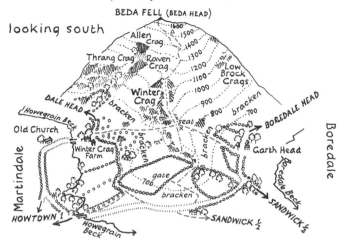

looking south

BEDA FELL (BEDA HEAD)

The fell is best climbed along its north ridge, over the serrated crest of Winter Crag. The ridge may be gained directly at its extremity from the unenclosed road curving round its tip (in high summer, this route involves a tussle with bracken) or by the short paths from Winter Crag Farm and Garth Head. The ridge of Winter Crag is very enjoyable, but the final slope is dreary, although it may be improved by keeping well to the left to look down the crags into Martindale.

DESCENTS : Use the routes of ascent for returning, unless an extension of the walk is desired, in which case the ridge may be continued south-west as far as the Patterdale-Martindale path and a descent made along it.

In mist, exceeding care is necessary to avoid getting entangled among the crags on the east (Martindale) flank, Allen Crag especially being dangerous. In such conditions, it is advisable to descend from the lower cairn, 150 yards northwest, keeping always to the ridge.

THE SUMMIT

The highest point, Beda Head, is an uninteresting mound set upon undulating grassy slopes. Infinitely more exciting and attractive is the rocky top of Winter Crag along the ridge.

THE VIEW

Principal Fells

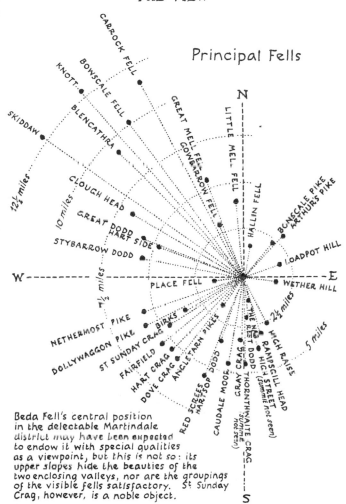

CARROCK FELL
BOWSCALE FELL
KNOTT
SKIDDAW
BLENCATHRA
GREAT MELL FELL
GOWBARROW FELL
LITTLE MELL FELL
N
HALLIN FELL
BONSCALE PIKE
ARTHURS PIKE
CLOUGH HEAD
12½ miles
10 miles
GREAT DODD
HART SIDE
STYBARROW DODD
LOADPOT HILL
W — — E
7½ miles
PLACE FELL
WETHER HILL
NETHERMOST PIKE
DOLLYWAGGON PIKE
BIRKS
ST SUNDAY CRAG
FAIRFIELD
HART CRAG
DOVE CRAG
ANGLETARN PIKES
HARTSOP DODD
RED SCREES
CAUDALE MOOR
GRAY CRAG
THE NEST DODD
THORNTHWAITE CRAG (summit not seen)
RAMPSGILL HEAD
HIGH RAISE
HIGH STREET (summit not seen)
2¼ miles
5 miles
S

Beda Fell's central position
in the delectable Martindale
district may have been expected
to endow it with special qualities
as a viewpoint, but this is not so: its
upper slopes hide the beauties of the
two enclosing valleys, nor are the groupings
of the visible fells satisfactory. St Sunday
Crag, however, is a noble object.

Lakes and Tarns
N to NE : Ullswater (two sections, divided by Hallin Fell)

RIDGE ROUTE

To ANGLETARN PIKES, 1857'
2 miles : SW, then S and SW
Main depression at 1450'
and several minor depressions

An easy walk on grass, increasing in interest
Follow the narrowing ridge southwest
along a sometimes intermittent
path. The first craggy rise, with a
cairn, is Bedafell Knott; beyond it
the main Patterdale-Martindale
path is crossed as it tops the ridge.
From the cairn above Broad Crags
a slight track skirts the eastern
edge of the ridge (striking
view of Heck Crag here).
The final rise ahead
may be avoided on the
right, aiming directly
for the main Pike
now in sight across
a depression.

*In mist, the latter
part of this route
(beyond the cross-path)
is not recommended*

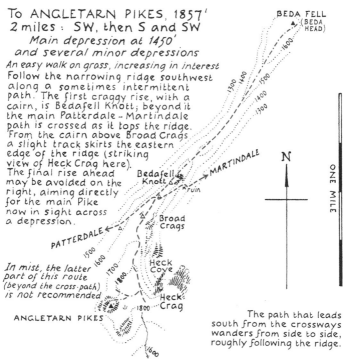

The path that leads
south from the crossways
wanders from side to side,
roughly following the ridge.

The ridge south from the cairn
above Broad Crags; on the right
the main Angletarn Pike.

Beda Fell
from
Martindale Old Church

Bonscale Pike 1718'

sometimes referred to as
Swarth Fell

from Hallin Fell

• Pooley Bridge

▲ ARTHUR'S PIKE
▲ BONSCALE PIKE
• Howtown

♦ LOADPOT HILL

MILES
0 1 2 3 4

NATURAL FEATURES

Rising steeply behind the little hamlet of Howtown is a broad buttress of the High Street range, Swarth Fell, the turretted and castellated rim of which has the appearance, when seen from Ullswater far below, of the ruined battlements of a castle wall: this aspect is sufficiently arresting to earn for the rocky facade and the summit above it the separate and distinctive name of Bonscale Pike. This escarpment, however, is a sham, for it defends nothing other than a dreary plateau of grass; and indeed there is little else of interest on the fell — excepting Swarthbeck Gill, its northern boundary, which abounds in interest but is out of bounds for the walker because of its obvious dangers. Bonscale Pike presents a bold front, that overlooking the lake, but on all other sides it loses its identity in the high mass of land supporting the great dome of Loadpot Hill.

MAP

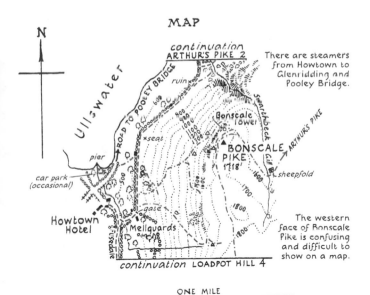

There are steamers from Howtown to Glenridding and Pooley Bridge.

The western face of Bonscale Pike is confusing and difficult to show on a map.

continuation ARTHUR'S PIKE 2

continuation LOADPOT HILL 4

ONE MILE

ASCENT FROM HOWTOWN
1200 feet of ascent : 1¼ miles

ARTHUR'S PIKE ←

sheepfold 1700

LOADPOT HILL →

LOADPOT HILL

BONSCALE PIKE

grass

Clumsy pedestrians should keep away from Swarthbeck Gill, which is dangerous.

Swarthbeck Gill

natural groove

groove

groove

1700

1600

1500

cairn on boulder

scree

1400

good path

1300

1200

1100

1000

bracken

ARTHUR'S PIKE and MOOR DIVOCK ←

bracken

bracken

900

800

700

seat ×

gateway

gate

Mellguards

FUSEDALE

gate

When the car park at Howtown is not operating it is best to park near the new church and use the pleasant path from there to Mellguards (*see the map on Steel Knotts 2*).

Howtown Hotel

looking east·south·east

The work of a craftsman
Bonscale Tower

The effort of amateurs
The higher pillar (now gone)

THE SUMMIT

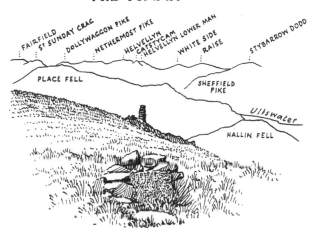

Two stone pillars can be seen prominently against the skyline from below. One of these, Bonscale Tower, has survived for over half a century; the other, ten yards to the east, is a newer construction. A cairn some 200 yards south of Bonscale Tower marks the site where a third pillar once stood. The highest point of the fell lies behind Bonscale Tower on a grassy hummock with a small summit cairn. It is an unsatisfactory summit because higher ground rises immediately beyond it on the long undulating slope to Loadpot Hill; it does, however, indicate an excellent viewpoint, and also defines the limit of interest, which is centred in the broken wall of crag immediately below. Bonscale Pike, in fact, gives a display of rock scenery that would improve many a bigger fell. And the men who selected the sites for the three pillars surely had a good appreciation of drama!

DESCENTS : None of the paths is easy to find.

In mist, a stranger may well feel cause for anxiety. Bonscale Tower should be rounded above it, by an ample margin, to reach the path below the crags, after which the slope may be safely descended anywhere if the path is lost. Note that the pillars stand on the brink of a crag. Resist any temptation to slant down to the stream: Swarthbeck Gill is highly dangerous.

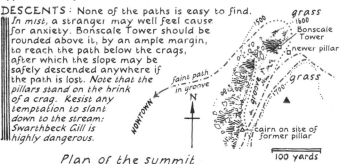

Plan of the summit

THE VIEW

Principal Fells

The distant fell peeping over the skyline, right of Arthur's Pike, is Cross Fell the highest of the Pennines

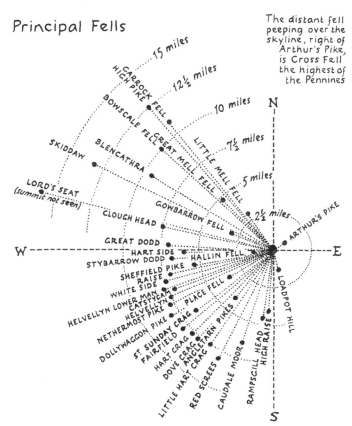

The prospect of the Helvellyn and Fairfield ranges, although crowded into a quarter-circle, is excellent, and the more distant northern fells are nicely grouped. In other directions there is little to be seen but the nearby dreary slopes falling from Loadpot Hill. The pillars are better viewpoints.

Lakes and Tarns

W to N: Ullswater
(middle and lower reaches)
– better seen from either
of the two pillars

RIDGE ROUTES

To ARTHUR'S PIKE, 1747': 1 mile
SE, then NNE and N
Depression at 1575'
200 feet of ascent

A simple walk, needing care in mist

Slant down a grass slope *south-east*
to the beck, crossing it above
a sheepfold and doubling back
along the opposite slope. There
are indistinct paths all the way
from Bonscale Pike to Arthur's
Pike. Short cuts across Swarthbeck
Gill, especially in mist, are dangerous.

To LOADPOT HILL, 2201': 1½ miles
S. then SSE and finally N
Minor depressions
550 feet of ascent

An easy walk, not recommended in mist

Cross the undulating plateau
southwards until the ground
steepens into the vast dome
of Loadpot Hill. A short climb
brings the old High Street (a
grassy groove) underfoot; it
leads to the ruins of Lowther
House, where turn north to
the handsome cairn.

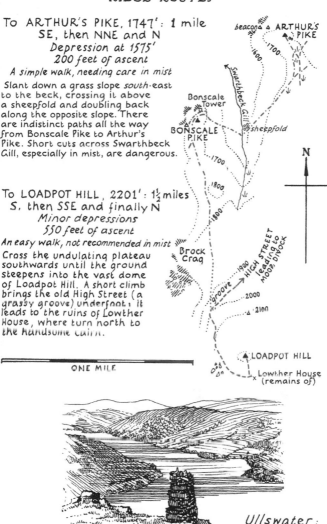

beacons △ ARTHUR'S PIKE

1700
1600

Swarthbeck Gill

Bonscale Tower

BONSCALE PIKE

sheepfold

N

1700

1800

1800

Brock Crag

groove

HIGH STREET leading to MOOR DIVOCK

1900

2000

△ 2100

LOADPOT HILL

Lowther House (remains of)

ONE MILE

Ullswater:
the middle reach

Branstree

2339'

(a corruption of Brant Street)

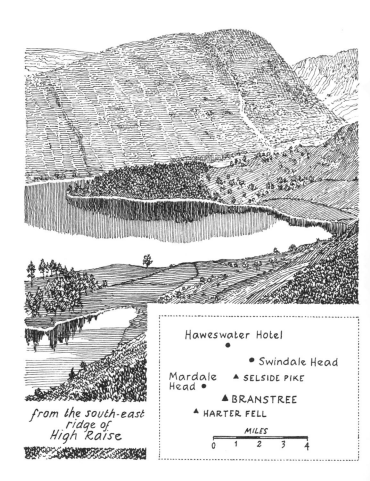

from the south-east
ridge of
High Raise

Haweswater Hotel
•

• Swindale Head

Mardale
Head •
▲ SELSIDE PIKE

▲ BRANSTREE

▲ HARTER FELL

MILES

0 1 2 3 4

NATURAL FEATURES

Branstree occupies a fine position at the head of three valleys, Mardale, Swindale and Longsleddale, and a fourth, Mosedale, runs along its southern base. This geographical attribute aside, the fell is dreary, and must disappoint all who climb it, for a good deal of perambulation is necessary across the flat and featureless top before these valleys can be brought sufficiently into view for full appreciation. All is grass, although there is a slight boulder-slope below Artlecrag Pike (extravagantly hachured as a crag on most maps), and a remarkable dry gully, the result of a landslide, cleaves the fellside on the Mardale flank from top to bottom. Eastwards there are some subsidiary summits, and a line of crags overlooking Swindale; there is an odd little hanging valley, and noble hidden waterfalls on this side. The Mosedale flank has been extensively quarried. Mosedale Beck is the principal stream : it runs into Swindale Beck. Manchester Corporation once coveted Swindale as the site of a proposed reservoir.

High Street
from the north ridge

MAP

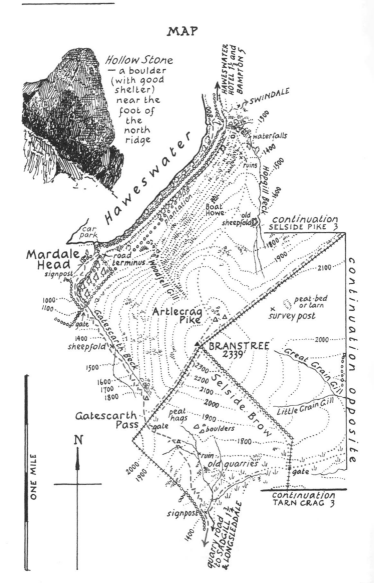

Hollow Stone — a boulder (with good shelter) near the foot of the north ridge

HAWESWATER HOTEL 1½ and BAMPTON 5

SWINDALE

waterfalls

ruins

Hopgill Beck

Haweswater

plantation

Boat Howe

old sheepfold

continuation
SELSIDE PIKE 3

car park

Mardale Head

signpost

road terminus

Woodell Gill

1000
1100

gate

1400
sheepfold

1500

1600
1700
1800

Gatescarth Beck

Artlecrag Pike

peat-bed or tarn
× survey post

BRANSTREE
2339'

Selside Brow

2300
2200
2100
2000

Great Crain Gill

Little Crain Gill

Gatescarth Pass

gate

peat hags

1900
boulders

ruin
old quarries

1800

gate

continuation
TARN CRAG 3

signpost

quarry road to SADGILL 1½ & LONGSLEDDALE

ONE MILE

N

continuation opposite

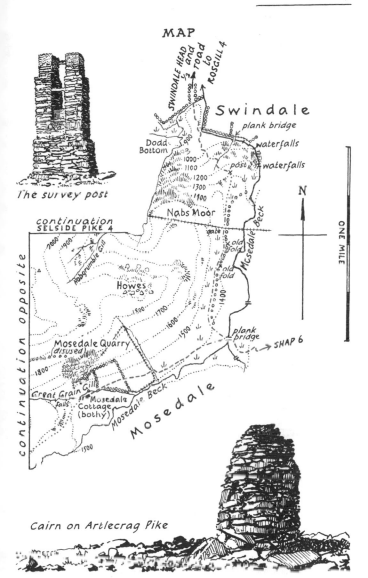

The survey post

MAP

SWINDALE HEAD and road to ROSGILL 4

Swindale

plank bridge

waterfalls

post

waterfalls

Dodd Bottom

1000
1100
1200
1300
1100

900

continuation SELSIDE PIKE 4

Nabs Moor

gate

old fold

Mosedale Beck

old fold

700
800
900

Hobgrumble Gill

Howes

1800
1700
1600
1500

1400

N

ONE MILE

plank bridge

SHAP 6

continuation opposite

Mosedale Quarry (disused)

1800

Great Grain Gill falls

Mosedale Cottage (bothy)

Mosedale Beck

Mosedale

1500

Cairn on Artlecrag Pike

ASCENT FROM MARDALE
1500 feet of ascent : 1½ miles from the road

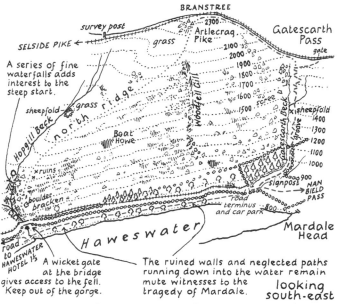

BRANSTREE

survey post

SELSIDE PIKE ←

grass

Artlecrag Pike

2300

Gatescarth Pass

gate

2100
2000
1900
1800
1700
1600
1500

A series of fine waterfalls adds interest to the steep start.

sheepfold — grass

north ridge

Boat Howe

Woofell Gill

scree

Gatescarth Beck

groove

sheepfold
1400
1300
1200
1100
1000

Hopgill Beck

×ruins

×boulder

bracken

900
signpost
NAN BIELD PASS

Road

terminus and car park

800

Mardale Head

road to HAWESWATER HOTEL ⅓

Haweswater

A wicket gate at the bridge gives access to the fell. Keep out of the gorge.

The ruined walls and neglected paths running down into the water remain mute witnesses to the tragedy of Mardale.

looking south-east

The merit of the ascent by the north ridge lies in its intimate views of Mardale Head and Harter Fell, the climbing itself being dull after a promising start. The Gatescarth route is better used for the return.

ASCENT FROM LONGSLEDDALE

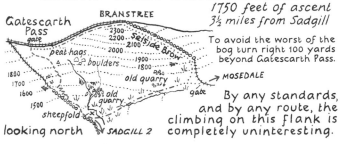

BRANSTREE

Gatescarth Pass
gate

2300
2200
2100
2000
1900
1800

Selside Brow

peat hags

boulders

old quarry

old quarry

1800
1700
1600
1500

sheepfold

looking north   SADGILL 2

1750 feet of ascent
3½ miles from Sadgill

To avoid the worst of the bog turn right 100 yards beyond Gatescarth Pass.

→ MOSEDALE

gate

By any standards, and by any route, the climbing on this flank is completely uninteresting.

THE SUMMIT

highest point

The 'official' watershed is about eighty yards north of the end of the wall; this is the highest point (2339')

The summit is grassy and flat-topped. The highest point is marked by a small cairn and an Ordnance Survey trigonometrical station, a circular structure about two feet across and two inches high with a small cone in the centre. A better place for a halt is Artlecrag Pike, nearby to the north-east; here there are two fine stone columns and some rock to relieve the drab surroundings.

DESCENTS : The quickest way off, and the safest in bad weather, is by the fence to Gatescarth Pass (keep to the right of the fence and watch for the gate that indicates the path for Longsleddale, left, and Mardale, right). The most attractive descent is that by the north ridge for Mardale, with good views of Haweswater.

RIDGE ROUTE

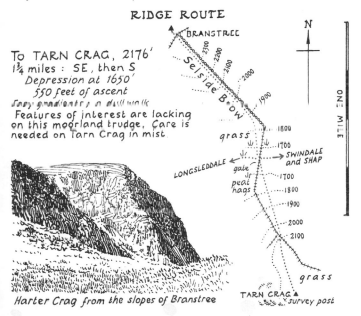

TO TARN CRAG, 2176'
1¼ miles : SE, then S
Depression at 1650'
550 feet of ascent
Easy gradients: a dull walk

Features of interest are lacking on this moorland trudge. Care is needed on Tarn Crag in mist.

N

BRANSTREE

Selside Bow

2300 2200 2000 2000 1900

1800

grass

1700

LONGSLEDDALE ← SWINDALE and SHAP

gate
peat
hags

1700
1800
1900
2000
2100

ONE MILE

grass

TARN CRAG ▲
survey post

Harter Crag from the slopes of Branstree

RIDGE ROUTES

To HARTER FELL, 2552': 2 miles: SW then NW and SW
Depression at 1875'(Gatescarth Pass): 700 feet of ascent
An easy walk on grass. Safe in mist, with care

Follow the right-hand side of the fence down to Gatescarth Pass, then take the path that cuts off the corner. Where the fence bends sharply left is the setting of the drawing that was used to introduce the author's television programmes in the 1980s (see Harter Fell 10).

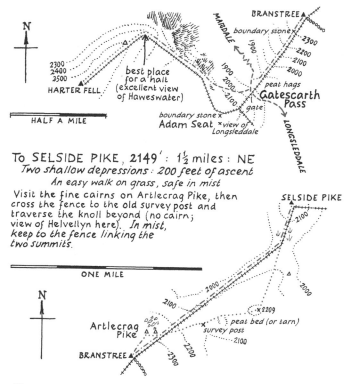

To SELSIDE PIKE, 2149': 1½ miles: NE
Two shallow depressions: 200 feet of ascent
An easy walk on grass, safe in mist

Visit the fine cairns on Artlecrag Pike, then cross the fence to the old survey post and traverse the knoll beyond (no cairn; view of Helvellyn here). *In mist, keep to the fence linking the two summits.*

The survey post was built by Manchester Corporation during the construction of the Haweswater Aqueduct. It does not stand on the crest of the depression, as might have been expected, but slightly below it; the top of the post, however, overtops the crest and the next survey post, on Tarn Crag, is visible from it (south).

THE VIEW

Principal Fells

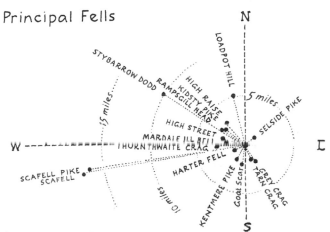

STYBARROW DODD
RAMPSGILL HEAD
KIDSTY PIKE
HIGH RAISE
LOADPOT HILL
N
15 miles
5 miles
HIGH STREET
SELSIDE PIKE
MARDALE ILL BELL
THORNTHWAITE CRAG
W
E
SCAFELL PIKE
SCAFELL
HARTER FELL
10 miles
KENTMERE PIKE
Goat Scar
GREY CRAG
TARN CRAG
S

Lakes and Tarns

Branstree is one of the very few Lakeland fells that have no view of lakes or tarns from the highest point, but Haweswater is brought into view by walking a few paces north. The long strip of water in the distance southwards is the Kent estuary.

Despite Branstree's good geographical position, little is seen of Lakeland: the lofty skyline of the Mardale heights admits only two small vistas of distant fells. Compensation is found, however, in the wide prospect of the Pennines. An interesting feature is the glimpse of the Scafells with Mickledore — note that, of this group, only the Pike is in view from the wall end.

Mosedale Cottage — now maintained as a mountain bothy

Brock Crags

from Goldrill Beck

Patterdale

ANGLETARN
▲ PIKES

BROCK ▲ CRAGS
● Hartsop

HIGH STREET ▲

MILES

0   1   2   3   4

The still unspoilt village of Hartsop has great charm and its environment is one of quiet loveliness, much of it contributed by the hanging woods of the steep fell that rises immediately behind. This fell, Brock Crags, is an offshoot of a ridge coming down to Ullswater from the main High Street watershed, and overlooks a meeting of many valleys: a feature in the view from the rocky top. Its slopes carry the Hayeswater aqueduct, and pipelaying operations there in the 1950s left an ugly scar along its fair breast. Nature is a great healer and it has healed effectively here.

MAP

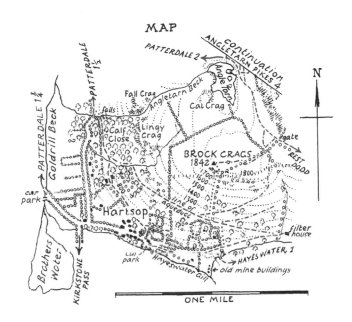

PATTERDALE 2

continuation
ANGLETARN PIKES 4

N

Fall Crag

Angletarn Beck

Angle Tarn

Cat Crag

falls

Calf Close

Lingy Crag

gate

BROCK CRAGS
1842

REST DODD

1700 1800

1600

1500

1400

line of aqueduct

1300

Hartsop

filter house

car park

Hayeswater Gill

HAYESWATER, 1

old mine buildings

Brothers Water

Goldrill Beck

PATTERDALE 1¾

PATTERDALE 1½

KIRKSTONE PASS

ONE MILE

ASCENT FROM HARTSOP
1300 feet of ascent : 1 mile

From the car park at Hartsop follow the road up the valley to the filter house, turning back along the pipeline at a higher level. Above the pipeline, find a grooved path ascending right through a gap in an old wall: it becomes indistinct at 1600, the summit then being over easy slopes to the left. Or follow the old wall straight up.

BROCK CRAGS

shelter
under crag
1500
1400
1300
1200

1800
1700
1600

old wall

grooved path

Hayeswater Aqueduct

pastures

1000 Pipeline

filter house

900

gate

800

Hayeswater Gill

Hartsop

gate

looking north

An iron gatepost, the sole remnant of a vanished fence, is to be found beside the grooved path at 1500'.

The scar left by the pipeline, which was once such an unnatural feature of the landscape, has now vanished without a trace.

THE SUMMIT

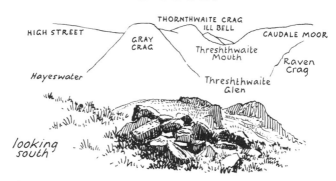

A series of rocky knolls, on the highest of which is a cairn, adds some interest to the rather drab surroundings. It is as a viewpoint that the summit merits most respect.

DESCENTS: A quick descent to Hartsop may be made by following downhill the old wall that crosses the fellside 150 yards south-east; descents due west encounter rough ground and should not be attempted. For Patterdale the Angle Tarn path may be joined near the Satura Crag gate by following the old wall eastwards. *In bad weather*, locate the wall and follow it down to the pastures of Hartsop.

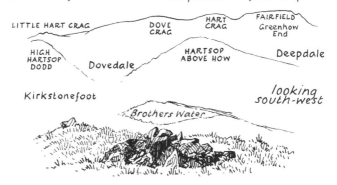

RIDGE ROUTES

Brock Crags stands apart from the ridge that links Rest Dodd with Angletarn Pikes. To join the ridge, for either of these fells, follow the old wall eastwards to the gate on Satura Crag, where the connecting path will be found.

THE VIEW

Principal Fells

The scene is interesting, with a fine surround of higher fells; in particular the bird's-eye view of Brothers Water and Hartsop is beautiful and dramatic

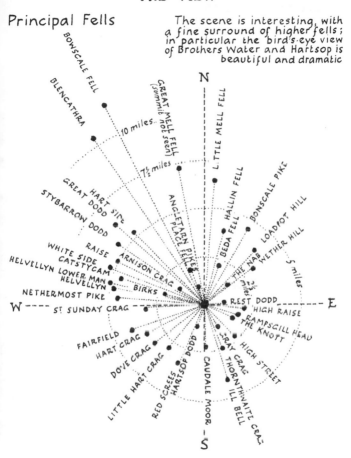

Lakes and Tarns

N : Angle Tarn
SE : Hayeswater
SW : Brothers Water
NW : Ullswater

Caudale Moor

2502'

often referred to as
  John Bell's Banner
summit named
  Stony Cove Pike

• Patterdale

• Hartsop

HIGH
STREET ▲

CAUDALE ▲ MOOR

▲ RED SCREES

• Ambleside

MILES

0 1 2 3 4

from Brothers Water

NATURAL FEATURES

Caudale Moor deserves far more respect than it usually
gets. The long featureless slope flanking the Kirkstone
Pass, well known to travellers, is not at all characteristic
of the fell : its other aspects, less frequently seen, are
considerably more imposing. There are, in fact, no fewer
than six ridges leaving the summit in other directions,
four of them of distinct merit and two of these rising
to subsidiary summits, Wansfell and Hartsop Dodd, on
their way to valley-level. The craggy slopes bordering
the upper Troutbeck valley are particularly varied and
interesting : from this remote dalehead Caudale Moor
looks really impressive, especially in snowy conditions.
The best single feature, however, is the formidable wall
of rock, Raven Crag, overlooking Pasture Beck. Of the
streams draining the fell, those to the south join forces
to form Trout Beck; all others go north to feed Ullswater.

looking west

1 : The summit (Stony Cove Pike)
2 : Hartsop Dodd
3 : St. Raven's Edge
4 : Main south ridge
    continuing to Wansfell
5 : Hart Crag
6 : Pike How
7 : Intermediate south ridge
8 : South ridge (east)
9 : North-west ridge
10 : North ridge
11 : East ridge
12 : Threshthwaite Mouth
13 : Raven Crag
14 : Woundale Beck
15 : Trout Beck
16 : Sad Gill
17 : Pasture Beck

The six ridges of Caudale Moor

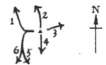

1 : North-west (to Brothers Water)
2 : North (to Hartsop)
3 : East (to Thornthwaite Crag
    or Hartsop or Troutbeck)
4 : South (east) (to Troutbeck)
5 : South (intermediate)
    (to Troutbeck)
6 : South (west) (to Kirkstone)

MAP

continuation on opposite page

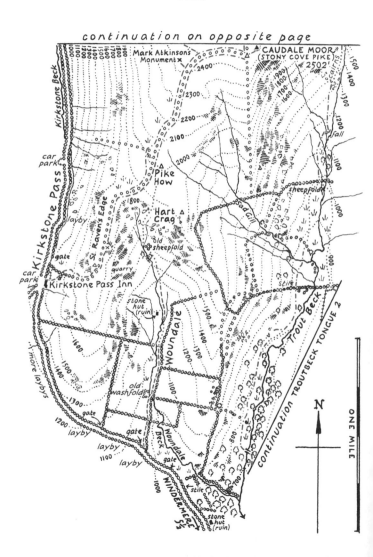

MAP

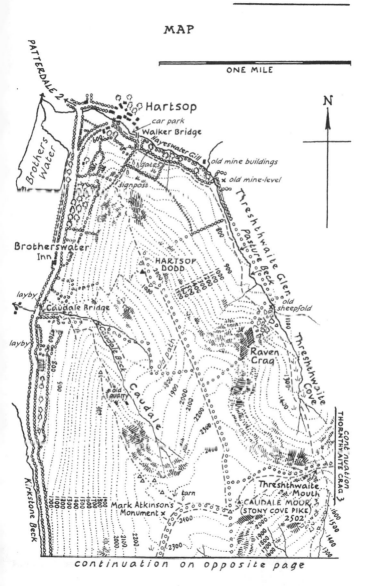

ONE MILE

N

continuation on opposite page

ASCENT FROM KIRKSTONE PASS
1150 feet of ascent : 2½ miles from the Inn

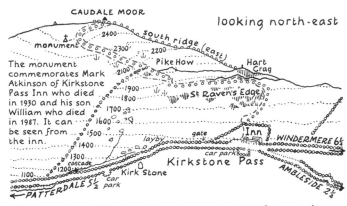

CAUDALE MOOR

looking north-east

2400

monument 2300

2200

south ridge (east)

Pike How

Hart Crag

2100

The monument commemorates Mark Atkinson of Kirkstone Pass Inn who died in 1930 and his son William who died in 1987. It can be seen from the inn.

1900

1800

St Raven's Edge

1700

1600

1500

1400

layby

gate

Inn

WINDERMERE 6½

1300

cascade

1200

car park

Kirkstone Pass

1100

Kirk Stone

←PATTERDALE 5½ car park

AMBLESIDE 2½

This route, with the advantage of a 1500' start, is one of the easiest ways up any of the higher fells, the only steep part being the short pull on to St Raven's Edge. It is also the *dullest* way up, and does not do justice to a fine hill that has much better than this to offer.

Caudale Moor from below Scot Rake

ASCENT FROM BROTHERS WATER
2000 feet of ascent : 2½ miles from the Inn

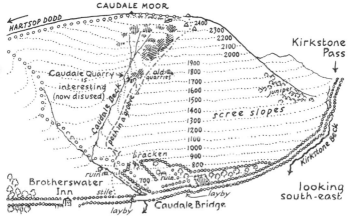

CAUDALE MOOR

HARTSOP DODD

△ 2400
△ 2300
2200
2100
2000

Kirkstone Pass

1900
1800
1700
1600
1500
1400
1300
1200
1100
1000
900
800
700

Caudale Quarry is interesting (now disused)

old quarries

path in a groove

Caudale Beck

scree slopes

juniper

Kirkstone Beck

bracken

ruin

ruin

Brotherswater Inn

stile

layby

layby

Caudale Bridge

looking south-east

The beautiful retrospect over Patterdale is justification for frequent halts during this continuously steep ascent. The route follows the well-defined crest of the ridge. Of the many approaches to the summit, this is by far the best.

Threshthwaite Cove from Threshthwaite Mouth

ASCENT FROM TROUTBECK
2200 (A) *or* 2350 (B) *feet of ascent:*
(A) *5 miles via Sad Gill; 5½ miles via Woundale* (A)
(B) *6 miles via St Raven's Edge or Threshthwaite Mouth* (B)

looking north

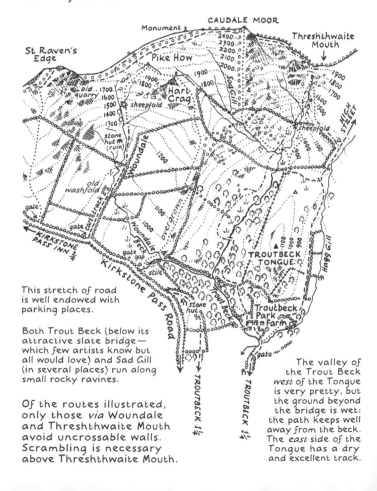

This stretch of road is well endowed with parking places.

Both Trout Beck (below its attractive slate bridge — which few artists know but all would love) and Sad Gill (in several places) run along small rocky ravines.

Of the routes illustrated, only those *via* Woundale and Threshthwaite Mouth avoid uncrossable walls. Scrambling is necessary above Threshthwaite Mouth.

The valley of the Trout Beck *west* of the Tongue is very pretty, but the ground beyond the bridge is wet: the path keeps well away from the beck. The *east* side of the Tongue has a dry and excellent track.

THE SUMMIT

KENTMERE PIKE   FROSWICK   ILL BELL   YOKE

The summit is a dreary plateau of considerable extent, crossed by ruined walls, with grey rock outcropping in the wide expanse of grass. The highest point is not easy to locate on the flat top: it is indicated by a cairn, *east of the north-south wall*, and bears the distinctive name of Stony Cove Pike.

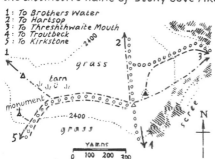

1 : To Brothers Water
2 : To Hartsop
3 : To Threshthwaite Mouth
4 : To Troutbeck
5 : To Kirkstone

grass
tarn
monument
2400
grass
5
N

YARDS
0   100   200   300

Mark Atkinson's Monument

Cairn above the north-west ridge

DESCENTS: All routes of ascent may be reversed in good weather. There are no distinct paths on the top, but broken walls offer safe guides from the summit except along the north-west ridge.

In bad weather, note that the east face is everywhere craggy: it may be descended safely *only* by the broken wall going down to the Threshthwaite gap. The best way off the top in an emergency, whatever the destination, is alongside the broken wall running west — this continues all the way to the road near Kirkstone Pass Inn.

THE VIEW

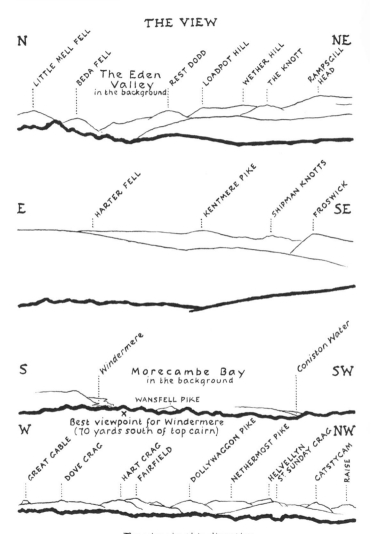

N — LITTLE MELL FELL — BEDA FELL — The Eden Valley in the background — REST DODD — LOADPOT HILL — WETHER HILL — THE KNOTT — RAMPSGILL HEAD — NE

E — HARTER FELL — KENTMERE PIKE — SHIPMAN KNOTTS — FROSWICK — SE

Windermere — Morecambe Bay in the background — Coniston Water

S — WANSFELL PIKE — SW

✕ Best viewpoint for Windermere (70 yards south of top cairn)

W — GREAT GABLE — DOVE CRAG — HART CRAG FAIRFIELD — DOLLYWAGGON PIKE — NETHERMOST PIKE — HELVELLYN St SUNDAY CRAG — CATSTYCAM — RAISE — NW

The view in this direction
is much better seen from
the western edge of the summit-plateau

THE VIEW

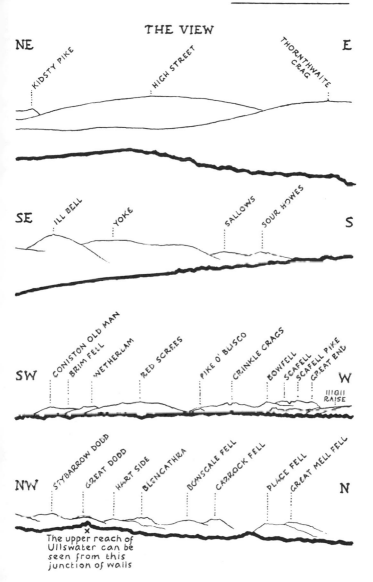

NE   E

KIDSTY PIKE   HIGH STREET   THORNTHWAITE CRAG

SE   S

ILL BELL   YOKE   SALLOWS   SOUR HOWES

SW   W

CONISTON OLD MAN   BRIM FELL   WETHERLAM   RED SCREES   PIKE O' BLISCO   CRINKLE CRAGS   BOWFELL   SCAFELL   SCAFELL PIKE   GREAT END   HIGH RAISE

NW   N

STYBARROW DODD   GREAT DODD   HART SIDE   BLENCATHRA   BOWSCALE FELL   CARROCK FELL   PLACE FELL   GREAT MELL FELL

The upper reach of
Ullswater can be
seen from this
junction of walls

RIDGE ROUTE

To WANSFELL, 1597': 4½ miles : W, then SW and S
Depression at 1100': 500 feet of ascent

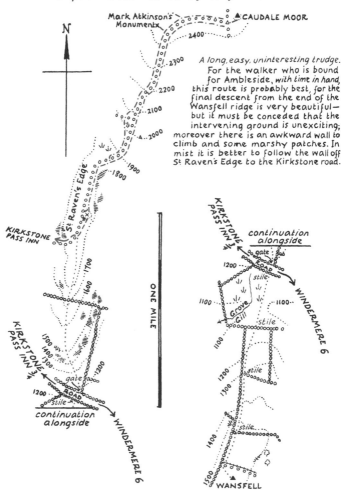

A long, easy, uninteresting trudge. For the walker who is bound for Ambleside, with time in hand, this route is probably best, for the final descent from the end of the Wansfell ridge is very beautiful — but it must be conceded that the intervening ground is unexciting; moreover there is an awkward wall to climb and some marshy patches. In mist it is better to follow the wall off St Raven's Edge to the Kirkstone road.

RIDGE ROUTES

To THORNTHWAITE CRAG, 2569': 1 mile: ENE, then E and SE
Depression at 1950': 620 feet of ascent
A rough scramble, safe in mist

This walk is not as simple as it looks, because the deep gap or col (Threshthwaite Mouth) between the two fells is unsuspected from the top of Caudale Moor. The descent to the gap is steep (if there is snow and ice it may be dangerous) and the climb from it is stony and loose. In mist, it is important to keep alongside the crumbled wall that links the two summits.

To HARTSOP DODD, 2028': 1⅓ miles: N, then NNW
Depression at 1900': 120 feet of ascent
An easy, straightforward walk

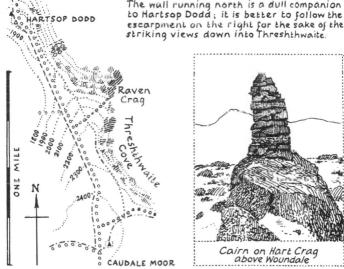

The wall running north is a dull companion to Hartsop Dodd; it is better to follow the escarpment on the right for the sake of the striking views down into Threshthwaite.

Cairn on Hart Crag above Woundale

Ullswater and Brothers Water
from Caudale Quarry

Red Screes and Middle Dodd
from the north-west ridge

Caudale Head

Raven Crag

Froswick

2359'

from Gavel Crag
(Ill Bell on the left)

▲ HIGH STREET

▲ THORNTHWAITE
     CRAG

▲ FROSWICK

▲ ILL BELL

▲ YOKE

Kentmere
•

• Troutbeck

MILES
0   1   2   3   4

NATURAL FEATURES

Sheltering in the shadow of Ill Bell on High Street's south ridge is the lesser height of Froswick. It takes its pattern from Ill Bell in remarkable degree, almost humorously seeming to ape its bigger neighbour. Both flanks are very steep, the Kentmere side especially being a rough tumble of scree: there are crags here facing up the valley. The grassy Troutbeck slope, west, is notable for Froswick's one touch of originality, for it is cleft by a tremendous scree gully, Blue Gill, that splits the fellside from top to bottom. Easy slopes link the summit with Thornthwaite Crag and Ill Bell; this is the finest part of the ridge.

MAP

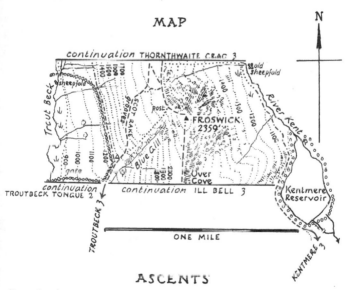

ASCENTS

Froswick is rarely climbed direct; invariably its summit is gained incidentally during the course of the Ill Bell ridge walk, starting at Garburn Pass. From Troutbeck, however, its top may be visited on the way to High Street by Scot Rake, in which case it is quicker to climb alongside Blue Gill than to waste time trying to locate Scot Rake. A direct ascent from Kentmere is not recommended, this flank being steep, loose and unpleasant, although the ridge north of the summit may be reached up a continuous tongue of grass from the sheepfold.

THE SUMMIT

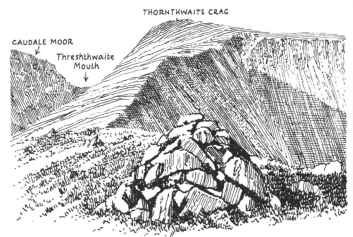

THORNTHWAITE CRAG

CAUDALE MOOR

Threshthwaite
Mouth

Froswick's peaked appearance from afar holds out the promise
of a small pointed summit. Small it is, and neat, with a tidy
cairn, but it will hardly satisfy the seeker of spires.
DESCENTS : The routes of ascent may be reversed. The western
flank is safe anywhere (but keep out of Blue Gill); do not attempt
the *direct* descent to Kentmere. *In mist*, reach Kentmere by way of
Garburn Pass.

RIDGE ROUTES

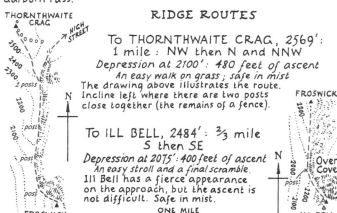

To THORNTHWAITE CRAG, 2569':
1 mile : NW then N and NNW
Depression at 2100': 480 feet of ascent
An easy walk on grass ; safe in mist
The drawing above illustrates the route.
Incline left where there are two posts
close together (the remains of a fence).

To ILL BELL, 2484': ⅔ mile
S then SE
Depression at 2075': 400 feet of ascent
An easy stroll and a final scramble.
Ill Bell has a fierce appearance
on the approach, but the ascent is
not difficult. Safe in mist.

ONE MILE

THE VIEW

Sandwiched between Thornthwaite Crag
and Ill Bell, both higher, Froswick
is an undistinguished viewpoint,
the best feature being the
serrated skyline of the
Scafell and Langdale
heights in the west

Principal Fells

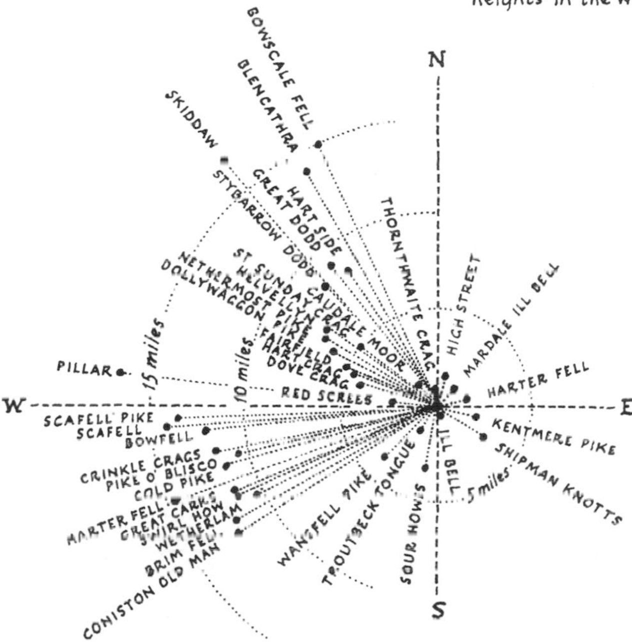

BOWSCALE FELL
BLENCATHRA
SKIDDAW
HART SIDE
GREAT DODD
STYBARROW DODD
ST SUNDAY CRAG
HELVELLYN
NETHERMOST PIKE
DOLLYWAGGON PIKE
CAUDALE MOOR
SEAT SANDAL
FAIRFIELD
HART CRAG
DOVE CRAG
RED SCREES
THORNTHWAITE CRAG
HIGH STREET
MARDALE ILL BELL
HARTER FELL
KENTMERE PIKE
SHIPMAN KNOTTS
ILL BELL
SOUR HOWES
TROUTBECK TONGUE
WANSFELL PIKE
BRIM FELL
WETHERLAM
SWIRL HOW
GREAT CARRS
HARTER FELL
COLD PIKE
PIKE O' BLISCO
CRINKLE CRAGS
BOWFELL
SCAFELL
SCAFELL PIKE
PILLAR
CONISTON OLD MAN

N
S
E
W

15 miles
10 miles
5 miles

Ill Bell
from
Froswick

Lakes and Tarns
SE : Kentmere Reservoir
SSW : Windermere
NNW : Ullswater

Gray Crag

2286'

Hartsop
▲ GRAY CRAG
▲ HIGH
STREET
THORNTHWAITE CRAG ▲

MILES
0   1   2   3

from Hartsop

NATURAL FEATURES

A lofty ridge, bounded by exceedingly steep flanks, extends northwards from Thornthwaite Crag with a slight curve to the west, and culminates high above Hayeswater Gill in a level platform from which, on both sides, fall precipitous crags split by deep gullies. This is Gray Crag, a prominent object in the Hartsop landscape. Hayeswater forms its eastern base, while the stream issuing therefrom defines it to the north. The western boundary, below an impressive cliff of shattered rocks, is Pasture Beck.

MAP

continuation
THORNTHWAITE CRAG 3

ASCENT FROM HARTSOP
1800 feet of ascent : 2 miles
(via Threshthwaite Mouth : 1950 feet of ascent : 4 miles)

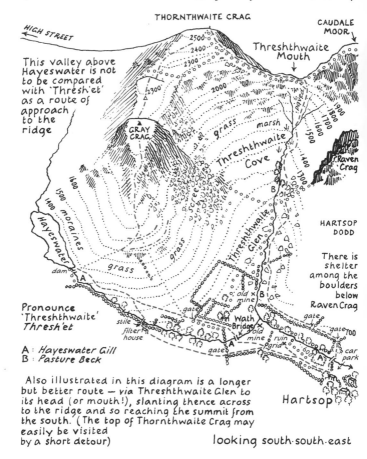

THORNTHWAITE CRAG

CAUDALE MOOR

HIGH STREET

Threshthwaite Mouth

This valley above Hayeswater is not to be compared with 'Thresh'et' as a route of approach to the ridge

GRAY CRAG

grass

marsh

Threshthwaite Cove

Raven Crag

Hayeswater

moraines

scree

grass

Threshthwaite Glen

HARTSOP DODD

There is shelter among the boulders below Raven Crag

dam

A

grass

Pronounce 'Threshthwaite' *Thresh'et*

A : Hayeswater Gill
B : Pasture Beck

stile
filter house

old × mine

gate

Wath Bridge

B

old mine

gate

ruin

grid

gate

gate

100

car park

A

Hartsop

Also illustrated in this diagram is a longer but better route — via Threshthwaite Glen to its head (or mouth!), slanting thence across to the ridge and so reaching the summit from the south. (The top of Thornthwaite Crag may easily be visited by a short detour)

looking south-south-east

The direct route climbs steeply to the ridge when free of the enclosing walls above Wath Bridge, but it is easier and more interesting to continue first to Hayeswater and gain the ridge from there.

THE SUMMIT

The summit is a pleasant level plateau of grass between steep cliffs, which should be visited for their striking downwards views. DESCENTS: The *only* practicable way off is by the descending north ridge. The path continues indistinctly to the foot of the hill, but the start of it is impossible to find in ascent. *In mist*, keep between the steep slopes (no rock has to be negotiated anywhere) until a plain path is reached *crossing* the fellside, and then another; *beyond* these, avoid a small crag and go down grass slopes to the Hayeswater path above Wath Bridge.

RIDGE ROUTE

To THORNTHWAITE CRAG, 2569'
1¼ miles : slightly E of S
Two minor depressions : 350 feet of ascent
A simple stroll on grass ; safe in mist

An indistinct path may be followed for much of the way. The escarpments on both flanks of the ridge are steep enough to warn of danger in mist, when it is necessary to note that *the first two walls are crossed at right angles and the third followed.*

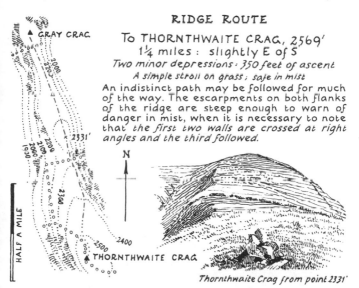

Thornthwaite Crag from point 2331'

THE VIEW

The edges of the escarpments are better viewpoints than the cairn, the steep declivities giving remarkable depth to the scene. While the view from the western edge of the summit is the more extensive, that from the eastern edge reveals the most striking picture, that of Hayeswater below.

Principal Fells

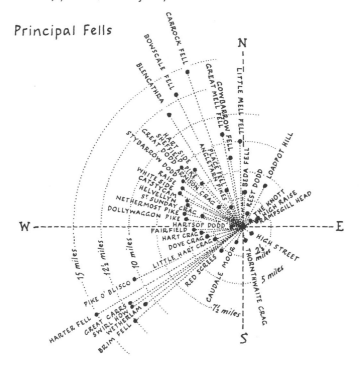

Lakes and Tarns

NNW : *Ullswater* (upper reach)

S : The small sheet of water seen above Threshthwaite Mouth is *Dubbs Reservoir*, Applethwaite Common. *Windermere* can be seen in the same direction by walking 300 yards along the ridge : it is especially well seen from point 2331. *Hayeswater* is brought into view by walking 50 yards in the direction of Rampsgill Head from the cairn, *Brothers Water* by walking 80 yards in the direction of Helvellyn.

Cascades above the filter house

Hayeswater Gill

Wath Bridge

Grey Crag

2093'

from Shipman Knotts

▲ HARTER FELL

▲ KENTMERE PIKE

▲ TARN CRAG

▲ GREY CRAG

road summit

Longsleddale

Huck's Bridge

Garnett Bridge

• Selside

MILES
0 1 2 3 4 5

NATURAL FEATURES

Shap Fells are the high link between the Pennines and Lakeland. They form a broad upland area of smooth grassy slopes and plateaux, inexpressibly wild and desolate but riven by deep valleys having each its lonely sheepfarm; gradually the ground rises in undulating ridges towards a focal point above the head of Longsleddale at the 2000-feet contour. The place of convergence of the ridges is Grey Crag, where is the first evidence, in rocky outcrops and low crags, of the characteristics so peculiar to Lakeland, although the influences of the Pennines persist in the form of peat-hags and marshes. These ridges, on a map, rather resemble the spread fingers and thumb of a hand, with Grey Crag as the palm.

1 : Grey Crag
2 : Tarn Crag
3 : Cappleburrow
4 : White Howe
5 : Lord's Seat
6 : Great Yarlside
7 : Wasdale Pike
8 : Seat Robert
9 : High Wether Howe

A : *Longsleddale*
B : *Bannisdale*
C : *Borrowdale*
D : *Crookdale*
E : *Wasdale*
F : *Wet Sleddale*
G : *Swindale*
H : *Mosedale*

There is nothing remarkable about Grey Crag, but here Lakeland may be said to start and moorland country to end — and the transition is sudden: the quiet beauty gives place to romantic beauty, placid scenery to exciting. One looks east, and the heart is soothed; west, and it is stirred. Longsleddale, at the western base of the fell, is a lovely valley and, at its head, typically Lakeland. Nearby, across a slight depression north-west, is a twin height, Tarn Crag; between them is Greycrag Tarn.

MAP

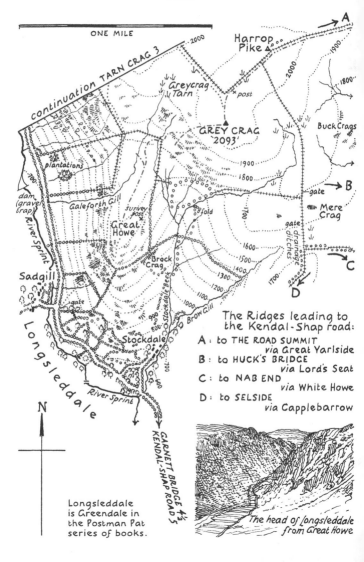

ONE MILE

continuation TARN CRAG 3

Harrop Pike △

Greycrag Tarn

× post

GREY CRAG 2093'

Buck Crags

1800

plantations

→ A
2000
1900
2000
1900

dam (gravel trap)

Galeforth Gill

survey post ×

fold

1900

1800

→ B
gate
Mere Crag
1700

River Sprint

Great Howe

Brock Crag

Stockdale Beck

Brow Gill

1600
1500
1400
1300
1200
1100
1000
900
800
700

gate
drainage ditches

→ C
1700

→ D

Sadgill

Longsleddale

gate

Stockdale

600
700

River Sprint

N

GARNETT BRIDGE 4½
KENDAL-SHAP ROAD 5

The Ridges leading to the Kendal-Shap road:

A: to THE ROAD SUMMIT
   via Great Yarlside
B: to HUCK'S BRIDGE
   via Lord's Seat
C: to NAB END
   via White Howe
D: to SELSIDE
   via Capplebarrow

Longsleddale is Greendale in the Postman Pat series of books.

The head of Longsleddale from Great Howe

ASCENT FROM LONGSLEDDALE
1500 feet of ascent : 1½ miles from Sadgill

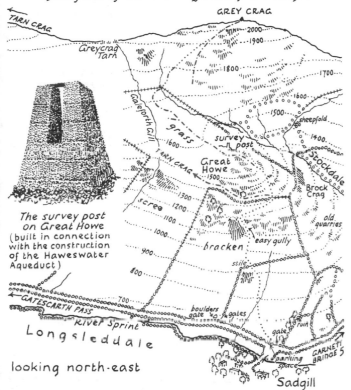

GREY CRAG

TARN CRAG

Greycrag Tarn

2000
1900
1800
1700
1600
1500
1400
1300
1200
1100
1000
900
800
700

Galeforth Gill

grass

survey post

Great Howe

Tarn Crag

scree

bracken

sheepfold

Stockdale

Brock Crag

old quarries

easy gully

stile

boulders
gate
gates

gate   ruin

GATESCARTH PASS

River Sprint

Longsleddale

looking north·east

parking space

GARNETT
BRIDGE 5

Sadgill

The survey post on Great Howe (built in connection with the construction of the Haweswater Aqueduct)

The hurdle across the gap in the wall at the top of the first enclosure was once awkward to negotiate, being too frail to climb. Ladies, and gentlemen with short legs, mindful of their dignity, will be glad to note that a stile has now been provided.

Great Howe is an excellent viewpoint for Longsleddale.

The ascent should be commenced from Sadgill Bridge, the more direct Stockdale route being much less attractive than the climb over Great Howe. The first thousand feet is steep. In mist, the ascent has nothing to commend it.

ASCENTS FROM THE KENDAL-SHAP ROAD

Grey Crag may be approached from the eastern fringe of the district along any of four clearly-defined ridges each of which has independent and distinct summits — and all of which descend to the main Kendal-Shap road. These approaches are described on this and the opposite page

1 : from   SELSIDE   and   NAB END
           1700 feet of ascent   1650 feet of ascent
              7 miles   6 miles

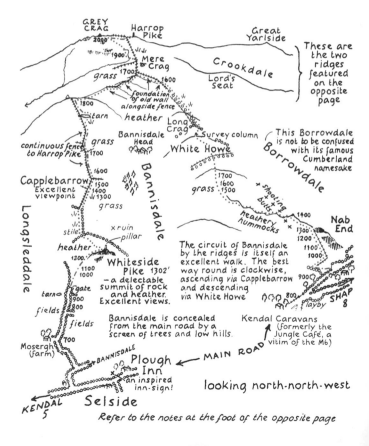

GREY CRAG
2000
1900
Harrop Pike
Great Yarlside

grass 1700 Mere Crag
1600
Crookdale
Lord's Seat

These are the two ridges featured on the opposite page

foundation of old wall alongside fence

1800
tarn
heather
Long Crag
Survey column
White Howe

continuous fence to Harrop Pike 1700
grass
Bannisdale Head
1700 1600 1500
grass

This Borrowdale is not to be confused with its famous Cumberland namesake

Borrowdale

Capplebarrow
Excellent viewpoint
1600
1500
1400
1300
grass
Bannisdale

shooting butts
heathery hummocks
1400 Nab End
1300
1200
1100
1000

Longsleddale

stiles
heather
x ruin
pillar

The circuit of Bannisdale by the ridges is itself an excellent walk. The best way round is clockwise, ascending via Capplebarrow and descending via White Howe

1200
1100
1000
Whiteside Pike 1302'
— a delectable summit of rock and heather. Excellent views.

900
800
SHAP 8
flayby

gate
tarn 900
800
fields
fields
700

Bannisdale is concealed from the main road by a screen of trees and low hills.

Kendal Caravans (formerly the Jungle Café, a victim of the M6)

Mosergh (farm)

BANNISDALE
Plough Inn
an inspired inn-sign!

← MAIN ROAD

KENDAL 5
Selside

looking north-north-west

Refer to the notes at the foot of the opposite page

ASCENTS FROM THE KENDAL-SHAP ROAD

2 : from HUCK'S BRIDGE and THE ROAD SUMMIT
1700 feet of ascent 1000 feet of ascent
5 miles 5 miles

looking
west·north·west

The Yarlside ridge is the easier
of the two illustrated; moreover, its
continuous fence makes it safe in mist.

It should be noted particularly that these routes lie across
very lonely territory; there are no paths along the ridges,
and visitors are infrequent. The desolation is profound. Solitary
walkers who want a decent burial should bear in mind that
if an accident befalls them in this wilderness their bones are
likely to adorn the scene until they rot and disintegrate.

These walks are more Pennine than Lakeland in character:
there is very little rock but much tough grass and heather, and
peat-hags and marshes are unwelcome features. Because of
the nature of the ground, the traverse of the ridges should be
undertaken only after a period of dry weather; they are best
left alone on a wet day or during a rainy season or if under
snow. Subject to the disabilities mentioned, it may be stated
at once that the ridges offer easy and exhilarating walking
in impressive surroundings, while the wide horizons and the
vast skyscapes deserve the brush of a Turner.

This is fine open country, but it is not Lakeland.

THE SUMMIT

The top of the fell is extensive, but the highest point, indicated by a cairn, is not in doubt although it stands but little above a wide expanse of small outcrops and peat-hags.
DESCENTS : In clear weather, with ample time in hand, a way may be made to the Kendal-Shap road by any of the four ridges. If Longsleddale is the objective, the descent should be made by Great Howe in preference to a direct route *via* Stockdale.
In bad conditions, the descent to the Kendal-Shap road must not be undertaken lightly. Note that only the Yarlside ridge has a continuous fence or wall all the way to the road.   For Longsleddale, *in mist*, pick a way straight down into Stockdale to avoid the scarps on Great Howe.

The cairn on Harrop Pike

Mere Crag

— a remarkably 'clean' face of rock, showing no sign of decay; lush grass grows up to its base. Climbers will enjoy its slabs.

RIDGE ROUTE
TO TARN CRAG, 2176'
¾ mile : N then NW and SSW
Depression at 1940':
250 feet of ascent
Straightforward walking, but it is better to skirt the marshes of Greycrag Tarn by keeping along the side of the fence.

N

2100
2000
2000
TARN CRAG
x survey post
peat hags
1900
Greycrag Tarn
GREY CRAG

HALF A MILE

THE VIEW

Grey Crag is the most easterly of the Lakeland fells, but is not of sufficient elevation to provide the panorama across the district that might be expected from its position. Higher neighbours around the head of Longsleddale conceal most of the better-known mountains, but the Coniston group is quite prominent and there is a peep of the Scafells over the saddle between Yoke and Ill Bell.

Principal Fells

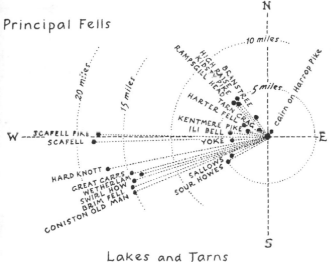

Lakes and Tarns

SSW : *Skeggles Water*
SW : *Windermere* (*two sections*)

Although the view towards Lakeland is disappointingly restricted, there can be no complaint of the quality of the prospects in other directions. On a clear day the panorama is remarkably extensive and very beautiful; there is a vastness, a spaciousness, about it that is usually lacking in the views from Lakeland summits. Just to the right of the cairn on Harrop Pike, Cross Fell and the twin Dun Fells start a glorious sweep of the Pennines extending south as far as Pendle Hill, with the principal heights of Mickle Fell, the Mallerstang fells, Whernside and Ingleborough all prominent. The nearer Howgill Fells, which always look attractive, are excellently grouped. Southwards is Kendal and the Kent Valley, and, beyond, Morecambe Bay silvers the horizon round to the isolated mass of Black Combe. There can be few better views in the country—but the days on which it is fully visible are also few, unfortunately.

Hallin Fell

1271'

from above Mellguards

Hallin Fell, beautifully situated overlooking a curve of Ullswater and commanding unrivalled views of the lovely secluded hinterland of Martindale, may be regarded as the motorists' fell, for the sandals and slippers and polished shoes of the numerous car-owners who park their properties on the crest of the road above the Howtown zig-zags on Sunday afternoons have smoothed to its summit a wide track that is seldom violated by the rough boots of fellwalkers. In choosing Hallin Fell as their weekend picnic-place and playground the Penrith and Carlisle motorists show commendable discrimination, for the rich rewards its summit offers are out of all proportion to the slight effort of ascent.

HALLIN FELL

● Sandwick ▲ ● Howtown

PLACE
FELL ▲   ▲ BEDA
              FELL

● Patterdale

MILES
0   1   2   3

MAP

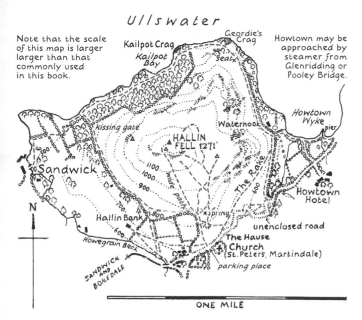

Ullswater

Note that the scale of this map is larger larger than that commonly used in this book.

Kailpot Crag
Kailpot Bay

Geordie's Crag

Seat

Howtown may be approached by steamer from Glenridding or Pooley Bridge.

kissing gate

Waterhook

Howtown Wyke

pier

HALLIN FELL 1271'

Sandwick

The Rake

Howtown Hotel

Hallin Bank

spring

unenclosed road

Howegrain Beck

The Hause
Church
(St. Peters, Martindale)

parking place

SANDWICK AND BOREDALE

N

ONE MILE

ASCENTS

There is one royal road to the top: this is the wide grass path leaving the Hause opposite the church, and it can be ascended comfortably in bare feet; in dry weather the short smooth turf is slippery. Another track from the Hause visits the large cairn overlooking Howtown, and offers an alternative route to the top. Incidentally (although this has nothing to do with fell-walking!) the lakeside path via Kailpot Crag is entirely delightful.

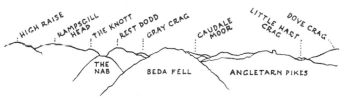

HIGH RAISE — RAMPSGILL HEAD — THE KNOTT — REST DODD — GRAY CRAG — CAUDALE MOOR — LITTLE HART CRAG — DOVE CRAG

THE NAB — BEDA FELL — ANGLETARN PIKES

The Martindale skyline, from the top of Hallin Fell

THE SUMMIT

The man who built the summit-cairn of Hallin Fell did more than indicate the highest point : he erected for himself a permanent memorial. This 12-foot obelisk, a landmark for miles around, is a massive structure of squared and prepared stone. Built into the cairn is a plaque bearing various initials and the date 1864. A small cairn, with a good view of the twin valleys of Boredale and Martindale, lies 70 yards SSW.

The top is mainly grassy with bracken encroaching ; there is a good deal of outcropping rock.

DESCENTS : The temptation to descend east directly to Howtown should be resisted for the slope above the Rake is rough and unpleasant.

The easiest way off, and the quickest, is by the path going down to the church on the Hause. *In mist, no other route can safely be attempted.*

The lower reach of Ullswater from north of the summit

THE VIEW

Principal Fells

The bird's-eye view of Ullswater is dramatic, but the classic scene unfolded is an intimate one of green fields and steep fells, the Martindale district, for which this is the best viewpoint. The panorama is good considering the modest elevation.

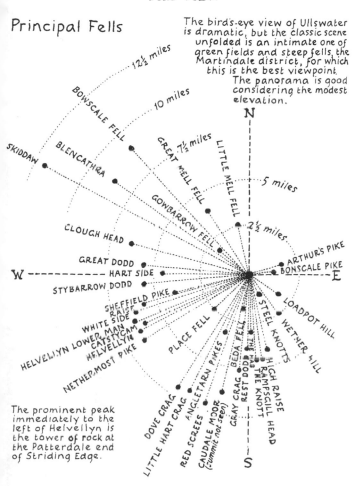

12½ miles

10 miles

BOWSCALE FELL

SKIDDAW

BLENCATHRA

GREAT MELL FELL

LITTLE MELL FELL

7½ miles

5 miles

GOWBARROW FELL

2½ miles

CLOUGH HEAD

ARTHUR'S PIKE

BONSCALE PIKE

GREAT DODD

W — — — — — — — HART SIDE — — — — — — E

STYBARROW DODD

LOADPOT HILL

SHEFFIELD PIKE

RAISE

WHITE SIDE

WETHER HILL

STEEL KNOTTS

HELVELLYN LOWER MAN

CATSTYCAM

HELVELLYN

PLACE FELL

HIGH RAISE

RAMPSGILL HEAD

THE KNOTT

NETHERMOST PIKE

BEDA FELL

REST DODD

GRAY CRAG

DOVE CRAG

LITTLE HART CRAG

ANGLETARN PIKES

RED SCREES

CAUDALE MOOR (summit not seen)

N

S

The prominent peak immediately to the left of Helvellyn is the tower of rock at the Patterdale end of Striding Edge.

Lakes and Tarns
WSW to NE : *Ullswater*
(all of the middle and lower reaches)

Harter Fell

HIGH
STREET ▲

Mardale Head
●

▲ HARTER FELL

ILL BELL
▲

▲ KENTMERE
PIKE

▲
SHIPMAN KNOTTS

● Kentmere

Longsleddale ●

MILES
0   1   2   3   4

from The Rigg

NATURAL FEATURES

A broad wedge of lonely upland country rises from
the valley of the Kent at Burneside and continues
north, narrowing, between the valleys of Kentmere
and Longsleddale for nine miles; until, having very
gradually attained its maximum height on Harter
Fell, the ground suddenly collapses in a tremendous
wall of crags, falling swiftly to the head of Mardale
amongst wild and romantic surroundings — one of
the noblest mountain scenes in the district. This
northern face is Harter Fell's chief glory, for here,
too, a shelf cradles Small Water, which is the finest
of Lakeland's tarns in the opinion of many qualified
to judge : seen in storm, the picture is most impressive
and awe-inspiring. The other slopes have less of note
although Drygrove Gill is an interesting example of
landslip and Wren Gill has extensive (and dangerous)
quarries. Harter Fell is one of the few fells that can
claim a well-known pass on either side of its summit:
Nan Bield Pass on the west and Gatescarth Pass on
the east link Kentmere and Longsleddale respectively
with Mardale, but since the hamlet of Mardale Head
was 'drowned' by Haweswater (shame!) these passes
have largely fallen from favour.

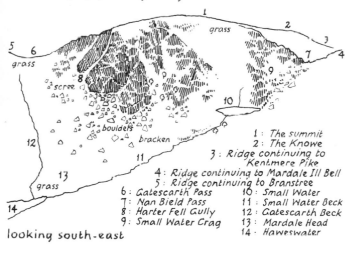

1 : The summit
2 : The Knowe
3 : Ridge continuing to
    Kentmere Pike
4 : Ridge continuing to Mardale Ill Bell
5 : Ridge continuing to Branstree
6 : Gatescarth Pass
7 : Nan Bield Pass
8 : Harter Fell Gully
9 : Small Water Crag
10 : Small Water
11 : Small Water Beck
12 : Gatescarth Beck
13 : Mardale Head
14 : Haweswater

looking south-east

MAP

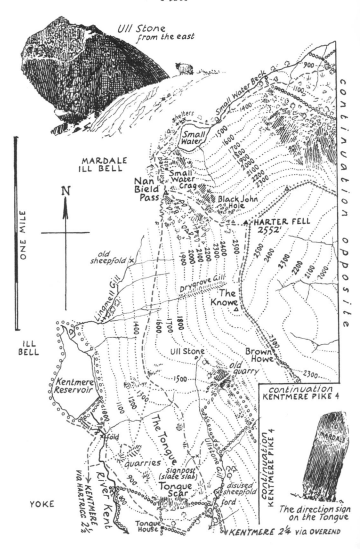

Ull Stone from the east

ONE MILE

N

MARDALE ILL BELL

ILL BELL

YOKE

Small Water Beck

shelters

Small Water

Small Water Crag

Nan Bield Pass

Black John Hole

HARTER FELL 2552'

old sheepfold

Drygrove Gill

The Knowe

Lingmell Gill

Brown Howe

Ull Stone

old quarry

Kentmere Reservoir

The Tongue

fold

quarries

signpost (slate slab)

Ullstone Gill

disused sheepfold

ford

Tongue Scar

Tongue House

River Kent

KENTMERE 2½ via HARTRIGG

KENTMERE 2¼ via OVEREND

continuation opposite

continuation KENTMERE PIKE 4

continuation KENTMERE PIKE 4

The direction sign on the Tongue

MAP

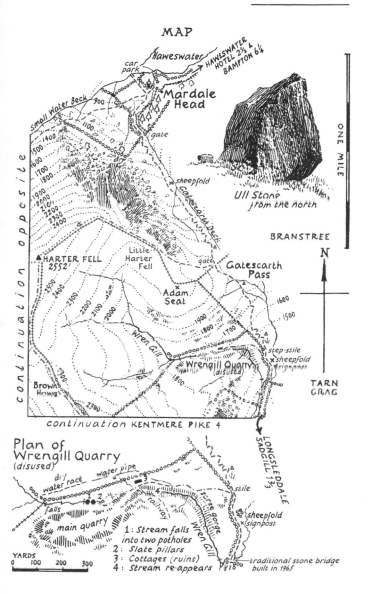

Haweswater

car park

HAWESWATER HOTEL 2¾ & BAMPTON 6¼

Small Water Beck

900

Mardale Head

1100

1400
1500
1600
1700
1800
1900
2000
2100
2200
2300
2400

gate

sheepfold

Gatescarth Beck

Ull Stone
from the north

ONE MILE

BRANSTREE

N

continuation opposite

HARTER FELL
2552'

2500
2400
2300
2200
2100
2000

Little
Harter
Fell

Adam
Seat

gate

Gatescarth
Pass

1600

1500

Wren Gill

1900
1800
1700

1900

Wrengill Quarry
(disused)

1800

step-stile
sheepfold
signpost

TARN
CRAG

Brown
Howe

2300

2300

continuation KENTMERE PIKE 4

LONGSLEDDALE
SADGILL 1¾

Plan of
Wrengill Quarry
(disused)

dry
water race   water pipe

falls

main quarry

stile

scree gorge

Wren Gill

sheepfold
signpost

YARDS
0   100   200   300

1: Stream falls
into two potholes
2: Slate pillars
3: Cottages (ruins)
4: Stream re-appears

traditional stone bridge
built in 1965

*The west face of Harter Fell
from the north-east ridge of Ill Bell*

ASCENT FROM KENTMERE
2200 feet of ascent
5¼ miles via Nan Bield Pass : 4¼ miles via Kentmere Pike

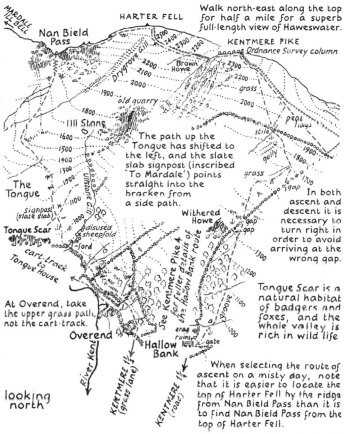

MARDALE ILL BELL

Nan Bield Pass

HARTER FELL

Walk north-east along the top for half a mile for a superb full-length view of Haweswater.

KENTMERE PIKE
Ordnance Survey column

Drygrove Gill

Brown Howe

grass

old quarry

Ill Stone

peat

stile

hags

gully

grass

The Tongue

The path up the Tongue has shifted to the left, and the slate slab signpost (inscribed 'To Mardale') points straight into the bracken from a side path.

In both ascent and descent it is necessary to turn right in order to avoid arriving at the wrong gap.

signpost (slate slab)

Tongue Scar

disused sheepfold

ford

Withered Howe

gap

gap

cart-track to Tongue House

See Kentmere Pike 4 for fuller details of the Hallow Bank route

Tongue Scar is a natural habitat of badgers and foxes, and the whole valley is rich in wild life

At Overend, take the upper grass path, not the cart-track.

Overend

Hallow Bank

ruins

gate

KENTMERE 1½ (grass lane)

KENTMERE 1½ (road)

When selecting the route of ascent on a misty day, note that it is easier to locate the top of Harter Fell by the ridge from Nan Bield Pass than it is to find Nan Bield Pass from the top of Harter Fell.

looking north

River Kent

Two routes are shown. That from Hallow Bank is both easier and shorter, that from Overend much the more beautiful and interesting. The round journey serves as an excellent introduction to upper Kentmere. The sharp-crested Nan Bield is the finest of Lakeland passes.

ASCENT FROM LONGSLEDDALE
1950 feet of ascent : 4¼ miles from Sadgill

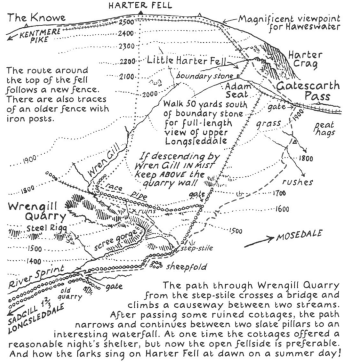

HARTER FELL

The Knowe

← KENTMERE PIKE

2500
2400
2300
2200
2100
2000

→ Magnificent viewpoint for Haweswater

Little Harter Fell

boundary stone

Harter Crag

The route around the top of the fell follows a new fence. There are also traces of an older fence with iron posts.

Adam Seat

Gatescarth Pass

gate

1900

grass

peat hags

Walk 50 yards south of boundary stone for full-length view of upper Longsleddale

1900

Wren Gill

1800

If descending by Wren Gill IN MIST keep ABOVE the quarry wall

race pipe

gate

1800

rushes

1700

Wrengill Quarry

Steel Rigg

ruins

1600

1500

scree gorge

→ MOSEDALE

1500

1400

step-stile

River Sprint

old quarry

gate

sheepfold

SADGILL 1¾
LONGSLEDDALE

The path through Wrengill Quarry from the step-stile crosses a bridge and climbs a causeway between two streams. After passing some ruined cottages, the path narrows and continues between two slate pillars to an interesting waterfall. At one time the cottages offered a reasonable night's shelter, but now the open fellside is preferable. And how the larks sing on Harter Fell at dawn on a summer day!

The disappearance of Wren Gill

looking north-west

The Gatescarth route is particularly easy: a hands-in-pockets stroll with no steep climbing, the top reached with surprising lack of effort. Nonagenarians will find it eminently suitable.
Avoid Wren Gill in mist.

ASCENT FROM MARDALE
1750 feet of ascent : 2 miles from the road end

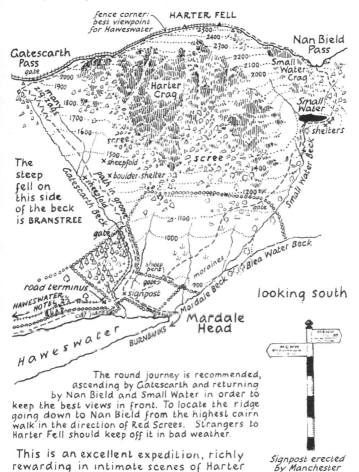

fence corner:
best viewpoint
for Haweswater

HARTER FELL

2500
2400
2300
2200
2100
2000

Nan Bield
Pass

Gatescarth
Pass
gate

Small
Water
Crag

Harter
Crag

2000
1900
1800
1700
1600

many zigzags

Small
Water

shelters

scree

1500
x sheepfold
x boulder·shelter

scree

path in groove
x sheepfold

1400

The
steep
fell on
this side
of the beck
is BRANSTREE

Gatescarth Beck

Small Water Beck

1200
gate

gate

1100

1000

sheep pens

moraines

Blea Water Beck

900
gate

road terminus
HAWESWATER
HOTEL

x signpost

Mardale Beck

looking south

car park

Haweswater

BURNBANKS

Mardale
Head

The round journey is recommended,
ascending by Gatescarth and returning
by Nan Bield and Small Water in order to
keep the best views in front. To locate the ridge
going down to Nan Bield from the highest cairn
walk in the direction of Red Screes. Strangers to
Harter Fell should keep off it in bad weather.

This is an excellent expedition, richly
rewarding in intimate scenes of Harter
Fell's grand northern cliffs and in the
views of Haweswater from its summit,
yet short in distance and needing much less effort in
execution than its formidable appearance suggests.

*Signpost erected
by Manchester
Corporation
Water Works*

THE SUMMIT

A mild shock awaits anyone reaching the top of the fell on a first visit, especially in mist, for there is a spectral weirdness about the two highest cairns. The stones support an elaborate superstructure of iron fence-posts and railings, which, having served their original mission, now act as an adornment that has a nightmarish quality.

The highest part of the fell, a graceful curve, is a long grassy sheep-walk. The pedestrian route across the top follows a wooden fence. As so often on easy ground, no paths have been trodden out, and only occasionally does a faint track materialise.

The fence corner is the setting for the illustration opposite, which was used to introduce the author's television programmes in the 1980s.

In mist, note the change of direction at the fence corner.

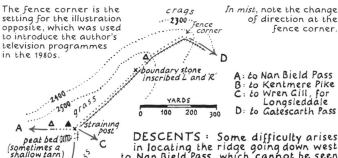

A: to Nan Bield Pass
B: to Kentmere Pike
C: to Wren Gill, for Longsleddale
D: to Gatescarth Pass

DESCENTS : Some difficulty arises in locating the ridge going down west to Nan Bield Pass, which cannot be seen from the summit. The top of the ridge is quickly reached by proceeding directly from the highest cairn towards Red Screes. Other routes follow the fence, although a quick way down to Wren Gill may also be noted.

In mist, aim for the Nan Bield ridge from the straining-post near the top cairn, passing between the cairn (right) and peat bed (left). Keep to the line of the fence on other routes.

Haweswater
from the fence corner

THE VIEW

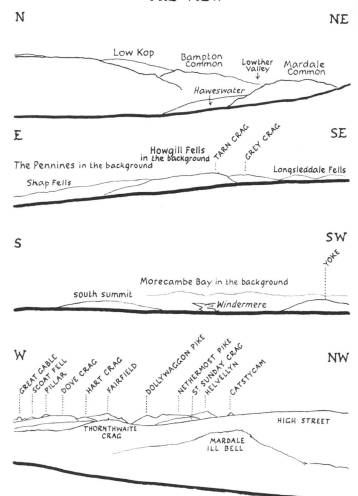

N — Low Kop — Bampton Common — Lowther Valley — Mardale Common — NE

Haweswater

E — The Pennines in the background — Shap Fells — Howgill Fells in the background — TARN CRAG — GREY CRAG — Longsleddale Fells — SE

S — south summit — Morecambe Bay in the background — Windermere — YOKE — SW

W — GREAT GABLE — SCOAT FELL — PILLAR — DOVE CRAG — HART CRAG — FAIRFIELD — THORNTHWAITE CRAG — DOLLYWAGGON PIKE — NETHERMOST PIKE — ST SUNDAY CRAG — HELVELLYN — CATSTYCAM — HIGH STREET — MARDALE ILL BELL — NW

THE VIEW

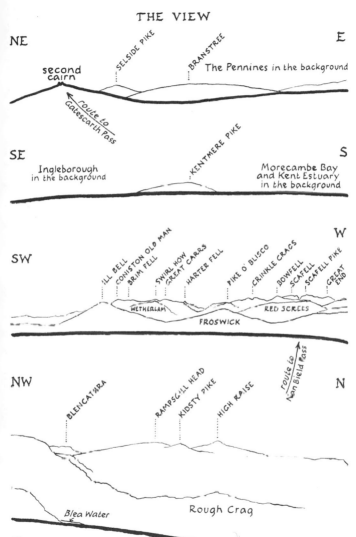

NE — second cairn · SELSIDE PIKE · BRANSTREE · The Pennines in the background · route to Gatescarth Pass — **E**

SE — Ingleborough in the background · KENTMERE PIKE · Morecambe Bay and Kent Estuary in the background — **S**

SW — 'LL BELL · CONISTON OLD MAN · BRIM FELL · SWIRL HOW · GREAT CARRS · HARTER FELL · PIKE O' BLISCO · CRINKLE CRAGS · BOWFELL · SCAFELL · SCAFELL PIKE · GREAT END · WETHERLAM · RED SCREES · FROSWICK — **W**

NW — BLENCATHRA · RAMPSGILL HEAD · KIDSTY PIKE · HIGH RAISE · route to Nan Bield Pass · Blea Water · Rough Crag — **N**

Blea Water cannot be seen from the cairn, but is brought into view by walking a few yards north-west.

RIDGE ROUTES

To BRANSTREE, 2339': 2 miles : NE then SE and NE
Depression at 1875' (Gatescarth Pass) : 465 feet of ascent
An easy walk on grass, tedious beyond Gatescarth

Follow the fence around the watershed to Little Harter Fell, where
a new path cuts the corner off to the top of Gatescarth Pass. Then
follow the fence up to Branstree. *In mist*, note the sharp angle in
the route after half a mile; crags are ahead.

To KENTMERE PIKE, 2397': 1¼ miles
S then SSE
Depression at 2275' : 150 feet of ascent
A simple stroll on grass

Follow the fence to the south along the ridge,
passing an iron post (the remains of a fence
which formerly ran down to the east).

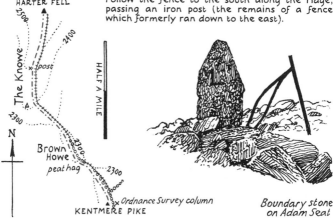

*Boundary stone
on Adam Seat*

RIDGE ROUTE

To MARDALE ILL BELL, 2496' : W, then WNW and NW
1 mile

Depression at 2100' (Nan Bield Pass) : 450 feet of ascent
An excellent crossing of a fine pass, with beautiful and impressive views
Aim west (in the direction of Red Screes) until the ridge going down
to Nan Bield is seen below: this is a delectable descent, Small Water
being a striking feature. Nan Bield is marked by a big cairn-shelter;
round the outcrop beyond on the left side. Slant up to the right over
rough ground when the path fades and watch for the white boulders
that indicate the final rise to the summit. *In mist, Mardale Ill Bell
is confusing and dangerous ; there are no paths across the top.*

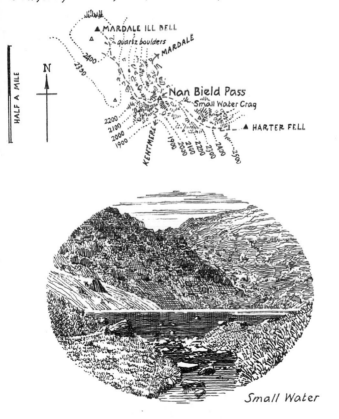

Small Water

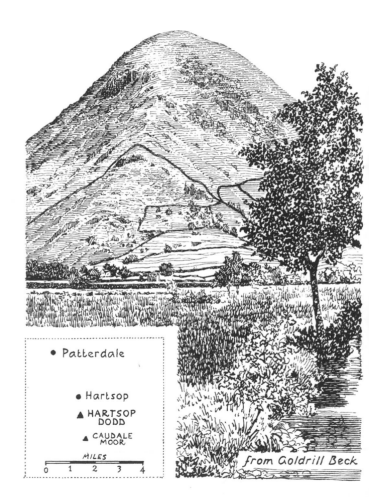

- Patterdale
- Hartsop
- ▲ HARTSOP DODD
- ▲ CAUDALE MOOR

MILES
0 1 2 3 4

from Goldrill Beck

NATURAL FEATURES

For a few miles along the road from Patterdale to Kirkstone, Hartsop Dodd has the form of a steepsided conical hill, rising like a giant tumulus from the flat floor of the valley; a high ridge connecting with the loftier Caudale Moor behind is unseen and unsuspected. After the fashion of many subsidiary fells in this area, the imposing front is a sham, for the Dodd is no more than the knuckled fist at the end of one of the several arms of Caudale Moor. It rises from pleasant places, pastures and woods and water, and quite rightly has been named from the delightful hamlet nestling unspoilt among trees at its foot.

It is interesting to note that Hartsop Dodd (*Low* Hartsop Dodd) has a greater elevation than its counterpart *High* Hartsop Dodd nearby, the prefixes relating to their geographical positions in the valley, not to their altitudes.

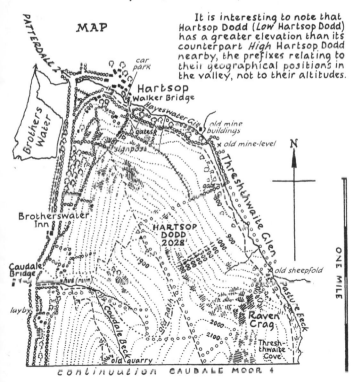

MAP

CONTINUATION CAUDALE MOOR 4

ASCENTS

A feature of the paths leading up Hartsop Dodd is that, for much of their length, they run in well-engineered grooves that help considerably in defining the routes. The best way up is by the steep north ridge, a beautiful climb. The path zigzagging up the west flank is now seldom used and is obstructed by bracken. The only easy route follows Caudale Beck at first and gains the ridge between the Dodd and Caudale Moor; this way is dull.

THE SUMMIT

The fence-post in the illustration is still there, although the wall has crumbled behind it. There is a cairn on the highest point, a large cairn on a prominent mound further to the north and another cairn to the south, by the first bend in the wall.

High Raise   Rampsgill Head   Gray Crag
The Knott

RIDGE ROUTE

HARTSOP DODD

Raven Crag

Threshthwaite Cove

ONE MILE

N

CAUDALE MOOR

DESCENTS : The grooves do not continue onto the summit. To find the path going down to the west, walk in the direction of Dove Crag, passing another fence-post minus fence — the top of the groove lies straight ahead. The path along the north ridge now leads to the car park at Walker Bridge. The old path from the ridge to Caudale Bridge (*marked on the map on Hartsop Dodd 2*) is to be preferred to the more direct route when the bracken is high.

In mist, the path on the west is very difficult to find — leave the top fence-post at right angles to the wall and look for a second post which gives the key to the descent.

To CAUDALE MOOR, 2502'
1½ miles : SSE, then S
Depression at 1900' : 620 feet of ascent

An easy climb on grass, safe in mist. The wall drearily links the two summits. In fine weather, interest may be introduced into the walk by following the edge of the escarpment on the left, the views therefrom down into Threshthwaite being very striking.

THE VIEW

The view of Dove Crag and Dovedale
across the gulf of the Patterdale valley
is exceedingly impressive, a classic
amongst views. Red Screes, too,
rises majestically and steeply
from the depths of Kirkstone.
The edges of the summit,
rather than the top,
give the best views.

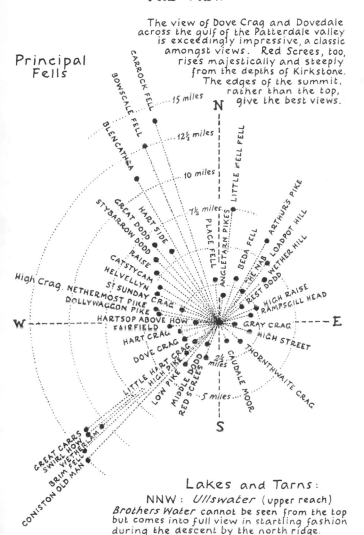

Principal Fells

Lakes and Tarns:

NNW: *Ullswater* (upper reach)
Brothers Water cannot be seen from the top
but comes into full view in startling fashion
during the descent by the north ridge.

Dovedale

Patterdale

High Raise

Howtown
Martindale
Bampton
▲ WETHER HILL
Measand
▲ HIGH RAISE
▲ HIGH STREET Riggindale

MILES
0 1 2 3 4

from the col
below The Knott

NATURAL FEATURES

Second in altitude among the fells east of Kirkstone and Ullswater, High Raise is overtopped only by High Street itself. Topographically, it cannot be said to occupy an important position, for it commands no valleys and it is not a meeting-place of ridges; yet, nevertheless, its summit-cone rises distinctively from the lofty watershed of the main range, and it is the last fell, going north, with the characteristics of a mountain — beyond are rolling foothills. Flanking it on the west is the valley of Ramps Gill, to which falls abruptly a featureless wall of grass and scree. Much more extensive, and much more interesting, are the eastern declivities, going down to Haweswater: here natural forces have scooped out a great hollow just below the subsidiary summit of Low Raise, leaving a mile-long fringe of crags between two airy ridges.
There are considerable streams on this flank, and all flow into Haweswater. Formerly these waters helped to irrigate the fertile Lowther and Eden valleys, but nowadays only the most favoured do so: the fate of the majority is captive travel along less pleasurable routes to the taps of Manchester, there to serve the needs of man in other ways.

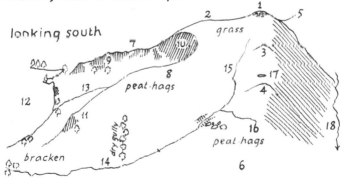

looking south

grass

peat-hags

peat-hags

bracken

dry gully

1 : *The summit*   2 : *Low Raise*   3 : *Raven Howe*   4 : *Red Crag*
5 : *Ridge continuing to Rampsgill Head*   6 : *Ridge continuing to Wether Hill*
7 : *South-east ridge*   8 : *North-east ridge*   9 : *Birks Crag*
10 : *Whelter Crags*   11 : *Lad Crags*   12 : *Haweswater*
13 : *Whelter Beck*   14 : *Measand Beck*   15 : *Longgrain Beck*
16 : *Keasgill Head*   17 : *Redcrag Tarn*   18 : *Rampsgill Beck*

MAP

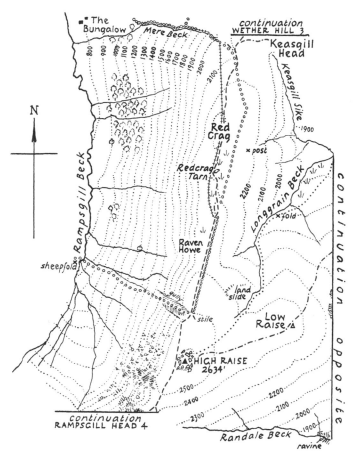

Ramps Gill is within the Martindale Deer Forest. Walkers are
requested not to enter this area (see The Nab 3)
to avoid disturbing the deer.

ONE MILE

MAP

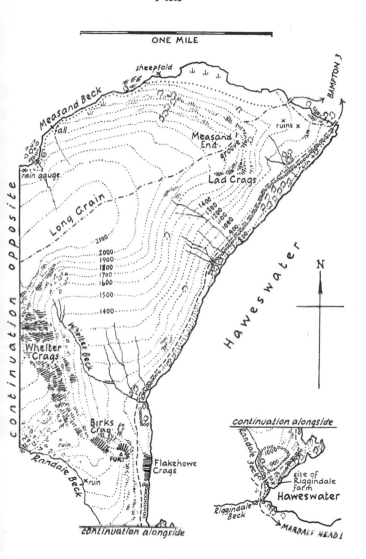

ONE MILE

ASCENTS FROM PATTERDALE AND HARTSOP
2400 feet of ascent : 5¼ miles from Patterdale
2250 feet of ascent : 3½ miles from Hartsop

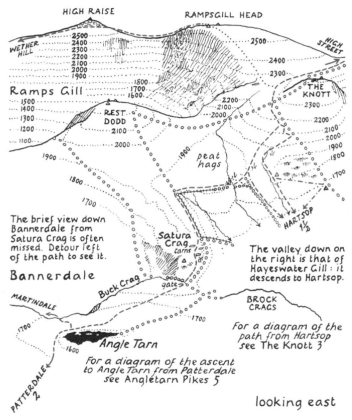

HIGH RAISE   RAMPSGILL HEAD

WETHER HILL

2500
2400
2300
2200
2100
2000
1900

HIGH STREET

2500

2400

2300

Ramps Gill

1800
1700
1600

1500
1400
1300
1200
1100

THE KNOTT

2300

REST DODD
2100

2200
2100
2000

2200

2100
2000
1900
1800
1700

2000

1900

1900

1800

peat hags

1700

The brief view down Bannerdale from Satura Crag is often missed. Detour left of the path to see it.

HARTSOP 1½

Bannerdale

Satura Crag
tarns

The valley down on the right is that of Hayeswater Gill : it descends to Hartsop.

MARTINDALE

Buck Crag

gate

BROCK CRAGS

1700

1700

Angle Tarn

1600

For a diagram of the path from Hartsop see The Knott 3

PATTERDALE 2

For a diagram of the ascent to Angle Tarn from Patterdale see Angletarn Pikes 5

looking east

This is a most enjoyable excursion with a succession of widely differing views, all excellent; and the route itself, never very distinct, is an interesting puzzle to unravel. In bad weather, however, there will be some difficulty, and a stranger may run into trouble on top of Rampsgill Head, where there are crags.

ASCENT FROM MARTINDALE
2100 feet of ascent : 5 miles from Martindale (Old Church)

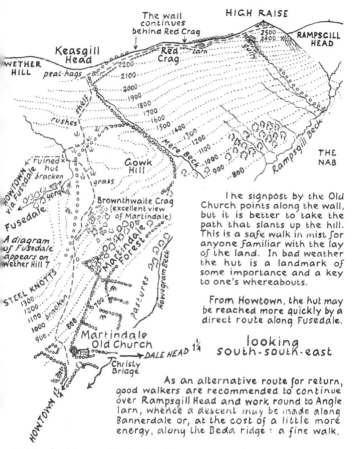

The signpost by the Old Church points along the wall, but it is better to take the path that slants up the hill. This is a safe walk in mist for anyone familiar with the lay of the land. In bad weather the hut is a landmark of some importance and a key to one's whereabouts.

From Howtown, the hut may be reached more quickly by a direct route along Fusedale.

looking south-south-east

As an alternative route for return, good walkers are recommended to continue over Rampsgill Head and work round to Angle Tarn, whence a descent may be made along Bannerdale or, at the cost of a little more energy, along the Beda ridge : a fine walk.

This is the only full-size mountain expedition conveniently available from the neighbourhood of Martindale and Howtown. It hardly lives up to its early promise, the middle section being dull, but the views are excellent throughout.

ASCENTS FROM MARDALE
1900 feet of ascent
3½ miles from Mardale Head ; 3½ miles from Measand

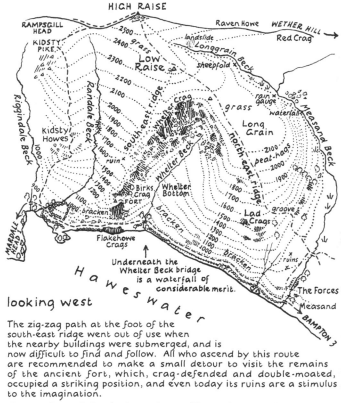

looking west

The zig-zag path at the foot of the
south-east ridge went out of use when
the nearby buildings were submerged, and is
now difficult to find and follow. All who ascend by this route
are recommended to make a small detour to visit the remains
of the ancient fort, which, crag-defended and double-moated,
occupied a striking position, and even today its ruins are a stimulus
to the imagination.

Much easier to follow is the path over Kidsty Howes, which has come
into use in recent years. At Kidsty Pike another path has to be found
which joins the ridge-path from Rampsgill Head to High Raise. The
best part of any of the routes is the path alongside the Forces on
Measand Beck, which is an endless succession of delights.

The routes along Measand Beck and over the south-east ridge
are unfrequented and without paths. All the routes are
interesting, and the ascent *via* the south-east ridge especially
is an attractive climb.

*Haweswater, from Measand
at the foot of the north-east ridge*

*The British Fort
on the south-east ridge
with Haweswater beyond*

THE SUMMIT

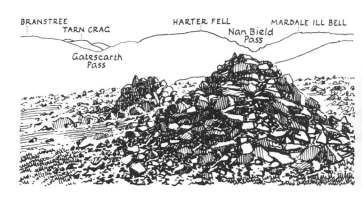

The true fell-walker appreciates best a summit with rocks; failing that, a summit with stones. He will, therefore, have an affectionate regard for High Raise, especially if his visit follows a tour of the neighbouring fells, for its top is crowned with stones in a quantity uncommon amongst the heights of the High Street range, which are usually grassy — they are rough, weathered and colourful stones, a pleasure to behold. Some have been used in the erection of a large cairn; others form an effective wind-shelter alongside. The old High Street, here merely a narrow track, crosses the top below the cap of stones, 100 yards west of the cairn. It is the only path.

A long half-mile away, slightly north of east, is the rounded hump of Low Raise. Here all is grass except for a remarkable oasis of bleached stones, obviously transported — a tumulus. These stones were a convenient quarry for later generations whose preference it was to build cairns rather than tumuli, and a really handsome edifice has been constructed.

The tumulus and cairn on Low Raise

DESCENTS

Since the friendly inn and farmsteads of Mardale were so cruelly sacrificed for the common good (sic), the summit of High Raise has been remote from tourist accommodation. The only beds in Mardale are in the Haweswater Hotel, which is on the wrong side of the lake for walkers, and which, unlike the old Dun Bull, is much more a motorists' resort than a refuge for foot-travellers and shepherds.

Ample time should be allowed for descents, which are lengthy in all directions, and confusing in all directions except to the east, especially so in bad weather.

The natural inclination to scramble down into Ramps Gill must be resisted : this valley offers sanctuary for deer, and there is neither welcome nor lodging for two-legged animals.

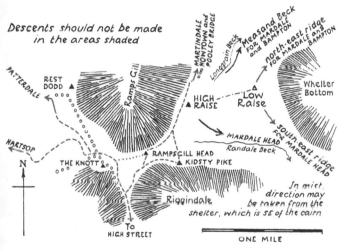

Descents should not be made in the areas shaded

In mist, direction may be taken from the shelter, which is SE of the cairn

ONE MILE

To PATTERDALE : An interesting and beautiful walk in good weather, but an anxious and complicated journey in bad. Note that Rampsgill Head must first be climbed before the descent properly commences, and that The Knott is rounded on its north side. *In bad weather, after crossing the wall between The Knott and Rest Dodd, descend directly to Hayeswater and Hartsop.*

To MARDALE : The north-east ridge particularly is a good way down, and the best if Bampton is the objective. The south-east ridge is rougher, with excellent views, but leads only to the uninhabited head of the valley : for the Haweswater Hotel, however, it is a useful route. *In mist, the streams are safe guides to the lakeside, but care is needed along Measand Beck.*

To MARTINDALE, HOWTOWN and POOLEY BRIDGE :   Follow the ridge north, turning down left at Keasgill Head for Martindale and Howtown — and, *in bad weather, for Pooley Bridge also.* Consult the Wether Hill map.

THE VIEW

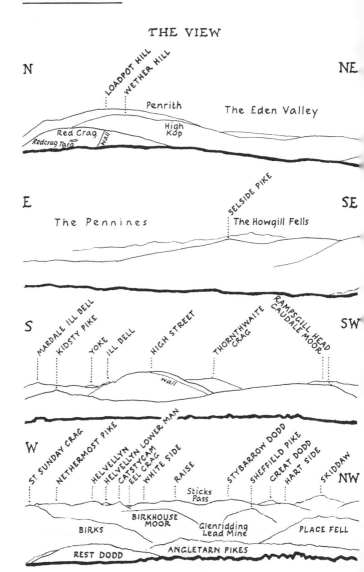

THE VIEW

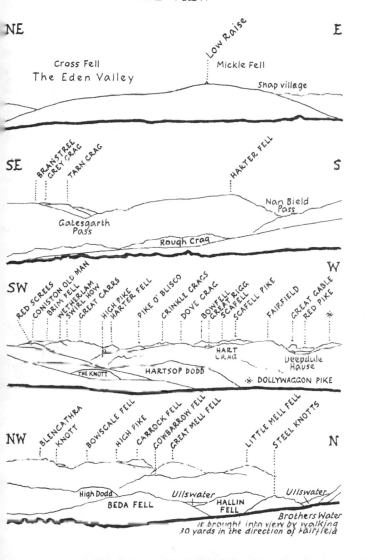

NE

Cross Fell
The Eden Valley

Low Raise

Mickle Fell

Shap village

E

SE

BRANSTREE
GREY CRAG
TARN CRAG

HARTER FELL

Gatesgarth
Pass

Nan Bield
Pass

Rough Crag

S

SW

RED SCREES
CONISTON OLD MAN
BRIM FELL
WETHERLAM
SWIRL HOW
GREAT CARRS
HIGH PIKE
HARTER FELL
PIKE O' BLISCO
CRINKLE CRAGS
DOVE CRAG
BOWFELL
GREAT RIGG
SCAFELL
SCAFELL PIKE
FAIRFIELD
GREAT GABLE
RED PIKE

HART
CRAG

Deepdale
Hause

THE KNOTT

HARTSOP DODD

✳ DOLLYWAGGON PIKE

W

NW

BLENCATHRA
KNOTT
BOWSCALE FELL
HIGH PIKE
CARROCK FELL
GOWBARROW FELL
GREAT MELL FELL

LITTLE MELL FELL

STEEL KNOTTS

High Dodd

BEDA FELL

Ullswater

HALLIN
FELL

Ullswater

Brothers Water
is brought into view by walking
30 yards in the direction of Fairfield

N

RIDGE ROUTES

To WETHER HILL, 2210': 2¼ miles : NNE
Depression at 2150' : 100 feet of ascent
A long easy walk, safe in mist

Facing north, incline left to join the path (the old High Street), which continues to Wether Hill and beyond. The course of the path has changed considerably in recent times and it is reasonable to assume that it has changed even more over the course of many centuries. It is known that the Roman High Street ran along the ridge, but it is unlikely that any of the paths currently in use follows it exactly

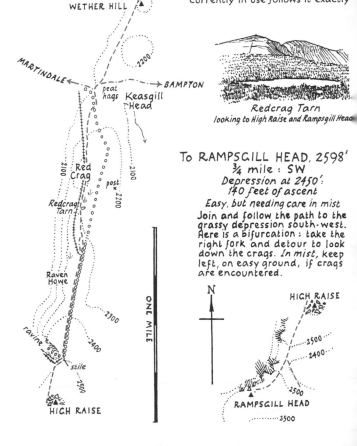

Redcrag Tarn
looking to High Raise and Rampsgill Head

To RAMPSGILL HEAD, 2598'
¾ mile : SW
Depression at 2450' : 140 feet of ascent
Easy, but needing care in mist

Join and follow the path to the grassy depression south-west. Here is a bifurcation: take the right fork and detour to look down the crags. In mist, keep left, on easy ground, if crags are encountered.

Whelter Beck and Whelter Crags

High Street

2718'

from the north ridge of Branstree

NATURAL FEATURES

- Patterdale

Hartsop

RAMPSGILL ▲ HEAD

▲ KIDSTY PIKE

HIGH ▲ STREET

THORNTHWAITE CRAG ▲   Mardale Head ●

▲ HARTER FELL

ILL BELL ▲

Kentmere ●
● Troutbeck

MILES

0   1   2   3   4

Most of the high places in Lakeland have no mention in history books, and, until comparatively recent times, when enlightened men were inspired to climb upon them for pleasure and exercise, it was fashionable to regard them as objects of awe and terror, and their summits were rarely visited.   Not so High Street, which has been known and trodden, down through the ages, by a miscellany of travellers on an odd variety of missions: by marching soldiers, marauding brigands, carousing shepherds, officials of the Governments, and now by modern hikers. Its summit has been in turn a highway and a sports arena and a racecourse, as well as, as it is today, a grazing ground for sheep.

The long whale-backed crest of High Street attains a greater altitude than any other fell east of Kirkstone. Walking is easy on the grassy top: a factor that must have influenced the Roman surveyors to throw their road along it.   But High Street is much more than an elevated and featureless field, for its eastern flank, which falls precipitously from the flat top to enclose the splendid tarn of Blea Water in craggy arms, is a striking study in grandeur and wildness; on this side a straight narrow ridge running down to Mardale is particularly fine.   The western face drops roughly to Hayeswater.   To north and south, high ground continues to subsidiary fells along the main ridge.

Rough Crag
from
Long Stile

The River Kent has its birth in marshes on the south slope but most of the water draining from the fell flows northwards to Haweswater and Hayeswater.

NATURAL FEATURES

The main High Street range
illustrating the complexity of the valley systems

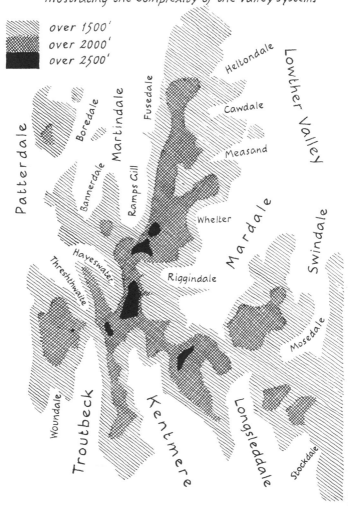

over 1500'
over 2000'
over 2500'

Lowther Valley

Heltondale

Cawdale

Patterdale

Boredale

Martindale

Fusedale

Measand

Bannerdale

Ramps Gill

Whelter

Mardale

Swindale

Hayeswater

Riggindale

Threshthwaite

Mosedale

Woundale

Troutbeck

Kentmere

Longsleddale

Stockdale

MAP

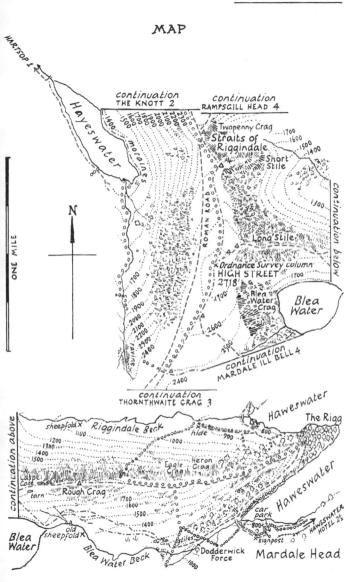

ASCENTS FROM PATTERDALE AND HARTSOP
2450 feet of ascent : 5½ miles from Patterdale
2300 feet of ascent : 3¾ miles from Hartsop

Proceed from the Straits of Riggindale to the summit
not by the wall nor by the Roman Road (which are
dull trudges) but by following the edge of the eastern
face (which has excellent views) until the Ordnance
Survey column comes into sight.

Enterprising pedestrians
approaching from Hartsop
may tackle High Street
direct from the head
of Hayeswater — but
they will not enjoy
the climb, which is
steep, dull, and
overburdened
with
scree.

For a diagram
of the path from
Hartsop to Hayeswater
see The Knott 3

For a diagram
of the ascent
to Angle Tarn
from Patterdale
see Angletarn Pikes 5

looking south-east

Two good viewpoints, only a few paces from the
path but often missed, are (1) the main cairn on
Satura Crag (view of Bannerdale), and (2) the tarn
on the col below Rampsgill Head (view of Ramps Gill)

This is the least exciting approach to High Street; it
is, nevertheless, a very enjoyable walk, with a series
of varied and beautiful views; and the tracking of
the indistinct path, which has many unexpected
turns and twists, is interesting throughout.

ASCENT FROM MARDALE

2050 feet of ascent   *3 miles from the road end*

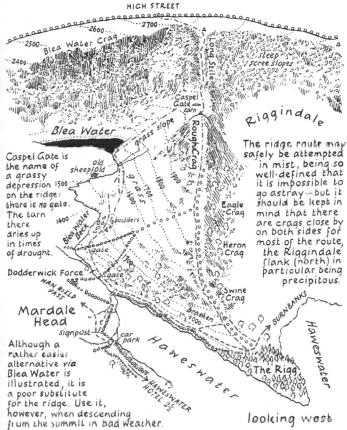

HIGH STREET

HIGH STREET

2600   2700

2500   Blea Water Crag

2400

Long Stile

steep scree slopes

Caspel Gate tarn

Blea Water

grass slope

Rough Crag

Riggindale

Caspel Gate is the name of a grassy depression *1500* on the ridge: there is no gate. The tarn there dries up in times of drought.

old sheepfold

grass

1800   1900

1700

1400   1600

Blea Water Beck   boulders

gate   1500

Eagle Crag

Heron Crag

The ridge route may safely be attempted in mist, being so well-defined that it is impossible to go astray — but it should be kept in mind that there are crags close by on both sides for most of the route, the Riggindale flank (north) in particular being precipitous.

Dodderwick Force

NAN BIELD PASS

gate

Swine Crag

bracken   1200

BURNBANKS

Mardale Head

signpost

car park

Haweswater

Haweswater

Although a rather easier alternative *via* Blea Water is illustrated, it is a poor substitute for the ridge. Use it, however, when descending from the summit in bad weather.

HAWESWATER HOTEL 2½

The Rigg

looking west

The ridge of Rough Crag and the rocky stairway of Long Stile together form the connoisseur's route up High Street, the only route that discloses the finer characteristics of the fell. The ascent is a classic, leading directly along the crest of a long, straight ridge that permits of no variation from the valley to the summit. The views are excellent throughout.

ASCENT FROM TROUTBECK
2350 feet of ascent : 6 miles

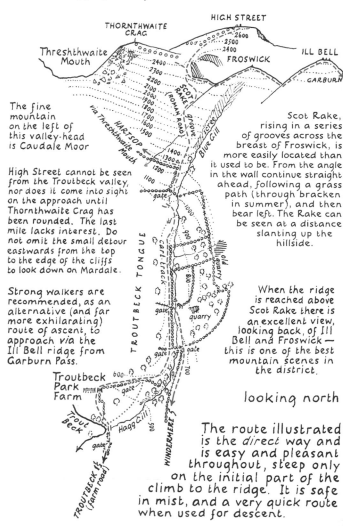

The fine mountain on the left of this valley-head is Caudale Moor

High Street cannot be seen from the Troutbeck valley, nor does it come into sight on the approach until Thornthwaite Crag has been rounded. The last mile lacks interest. Do not omit the small detour eastwards from the top to the edge of the cliffs to look down on Mardale.

Strong walkers are recommended, as an alternative (and far more exhilarating) route of ascent, to approach via the Ill Bell ridge from Garburn Pass.

Scot Rake, rising in a series of grooves across the breast of Froswick, is more easily located than it used to be. From the angle in the wall continue straight ahead, following a grass path (through bracken in summer), and then bear left. The Rake can be seen at a distance slanting up the hillside.

When the ridge is reached above Scot Rake there is an excellent view, looking back, of Ill Bell and Froswick — this is one of the best mountain scenes in the district.

looking north

The route illustrated is the *direct* way and is easy and pleasant throughout, steep only on the initial part of the climb to the ridge. It is safe in mist, and a very quick route when used for descent.

ASCENT FROM KENTMERE
2300 feet of ascent
5½ miles via Hall Cove : 6 miles via Nan Bield Pass

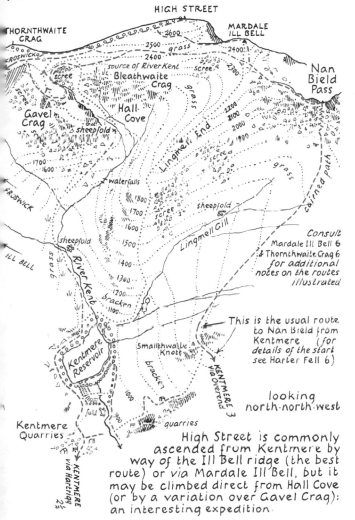

HIGH STREET

THORNTHWAITE CRAG

MARDALE ILL BELL

Nan Bield Pass

FROSWICK

source of River Kent

Bleathwaite Crag

Gavel Crag

Hall Cove

sheepfold

Lingmell End

scree

grass

scree

scree

grass

1700
1600

waterfalls

1800
1700
scree
1600
1500
1400
1300
1200
1100

sheepfold

FROSWICK

ILL BELL

sheepfold

grass

River Kent

Lingmell Gill

grass

cairned path

Consult Mardale Ill Bell 6 & Thornthwaite Crag 6 for additional notes on the routes illustrated

bracken

Kentmere Reservoir

Smallthwaite Knott

KENTMERE via Overend

This is the usual route to Nan Bield from Kentmere (for details of the start see Harter Fell 6)

looking north-north-west

bracken

Kentmere Quarries

KENTMERE via Hartrigg 2½

quarries

KENTMERE 3

High Street is commonly ascended from Kentmere by way of the Ill Bell ridge (the best route) or via Mardale Ill Bell, but it may be climbed direct from Hall Cove (or by a variation over Gavel Crag): an interesting expedition.

High Street 9

Haweswater, from above Long Stile

Hayeswater, from the Roman Road

THE SUMMIT

The summit is barren of scenic interest, and only visitors of lively imagination will fully appreciate their surroundings. Any person so favoured may recline on the turf and witness, in his mind's eye, a varied pageant of history, for he has been preceded here, down the ages, by the ancient Britons who built their villages and forts in the valleys around; by the Roman cohorts marching between their garrisons at Ambleside and Brougham; by the Scots invaders who were repulsed on the Troutbeck slopes; by the shepherds, dalesmen and farmers who, centuries ago, made the summit their playground and feasting-place on the occasion of their annual meets; by racing horses (the summit is still named Racecourse Hill on the large-scale Ordnance Survey maps).....and let us not forget Dixon of immortal legend, whose great fall over the cliff while fox-hunting is an epic in enthusiasm.

Nowadays all is quiet here and only the rising larks disturb the stillness. A pleasant place, but — to those unfortunate folk with no imagination — so dull!

DESCENTS should be made only by the regular routes. It must be emphasised that there is only one direct way to Mardale — by Long Stile, the top of which is indicated by a cairn. Direct descents into Kentmere may lead to trouble, the best plan being to aim for Nan Bield Pass, in clear weather.

In mist, consult the maps. For Mardale, stick to the crest of Long Stile, but at Caspel Gate turn down *right* to Blea Water. Kentmere is best reached by descending into Hall Cove at a point 100 yards south-east of the end of the High Street wall. Avoid the Hayeswater fare

N

HALF A MILE

broad path

High path

M

shelter cairn
column
main cairn

Roman Road

fold

Blea Water

M: Mardale
K: Kentmere
T: Troutbeck
H: Hartsop
P: Patterdale

Do not attempt descents in areas shaded

THE VIEW

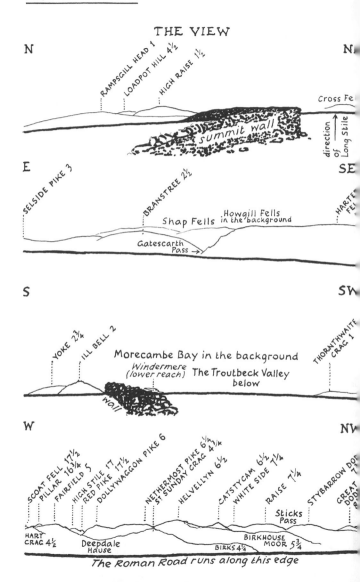

N

RAMPSGILL HEAD 1
LOADPOT HILL 4½
HIGH RAISE 1½

Cross Fe

N.

summit wall

direction of Long Stile

E

SELSIDE PIKE 3

BRANSTREE 2½

Shap Fells

Howgill Fells in the background

Gatescarth Pass →

SE

HARTE FEL

S

YOKE 2¾
ILL BELL 2

Morecambe Bay in the background

Windermere (lower reach) The Troutbeck Valley below

wall

THORNTHWAITE CRAG 1

SW

W

SCOAT FELL 17½
PILLAR 10¾
FAIRFIELD 5
HIGH STILE 17
RED PIKE 17½
DOLLYWAGGON PIKE 6
NETHERMOST PIKE 6½
ST SUNDAY CRAG 4½
HELVELLYN 6½
CATSTYCAM 6½
WHITE SIDE 7¼
RAISE 7¼
STYBARROW DO
GREAT DO

Sticks Pass

HART CRAG 4½

Deepdale Hause

BIRKS 4¼

BIRKHOUSE MOOR 5¾

NW

The Roman Road runs along this edge

THE VIEW

NE   E

The figures following the names of fells
indicate distances in miles

The Pennines in the background

View of Haweswater and Blea Water from this edge

SE   S

KENTMERE PIKE 2½ MARDALE ILL BELL ¾

Ingleborough

Morecambe Bay
and the Kent Estuary

The Kentmere Valley
below

SW   W

CONISTON OLD MAN 13¼
BRIM FELL 13
SWIRL HOW 12½
GREAT CARRS 12½
RED SCREES 3
HARTER FELL 15½
PIKE O' BLISCO 11½
CRINKLE CRAGS 12½
BOWFELL 12½
SCAFELL 14¾
SCAFELL PIKE 14¼
GREAT END 13½
GREAT GABLE 14½

DOVE CRAG 4

CAUDALE MOOR 1½

The Roman Road runs along this edge

NW   N

SKIDDAW 13¾
HART SIDE 7¼
ANGLETARN PIKES 3
BLENCATHRA 12½
PLACE FELL 4½
BONSCALE FELL 2¾
HIGH PIKE 16½
CARROCK FELL 15¼
REST DODD 1¾
GREAT MELL FELL 9¾
THE KNOTT 1
BEDA FELL 4
LITTLE MELL FELL 2

View of Hayeswater from this edge

RIDGE ROUTES

To RAMPSGILL HEAD, 2598' : 1¼ miles : N then NE
Depression at 2340' : 250 feet of ascent
An easy and interesting walk

Follow the edge of the escarpment north to the narrow Straits of Riggindale. Beyond, watch for the divergence to the right from the main path, and bear left when the top of the fell is reached.

To MARDALE ILL BELL, 2496' : ⅘ mile : SE then ESE
Depression at 2350' : 150 feet of ascent
An easy walk with fine views

Follow the edge of the escarpment south-east — the cross on the map marks an excellent view of Blea Water. Incline left when the marshy depression is crossed. In mist, it is better to use the path.

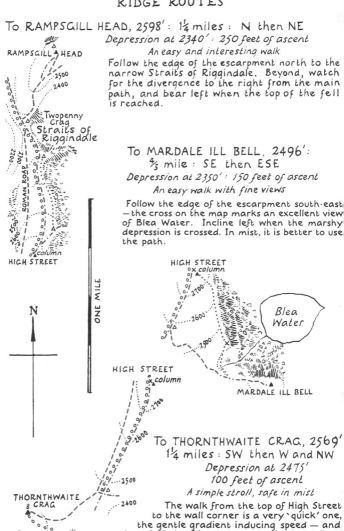

To THORNTHWAITE CRAG, 2569' : 1¼ miles : SW then W and NW
Depression at 2475' : 100 feet of ascent
A simple stroll, safe in mist

The walk from the top of High Street to the wall corner is a very 'quick' one, the gentle gradient inducing speed — and there is little of interest to detain the walker.

High Street from Mardale Ill Bell

Blea Water Crag

Ill Bell
2484

from upper Kentmere

▲ HIGH STREET
▲ THORNTHWAITE
CRAG
▲ FROSWICK
▲ ILL BELL
▲ YOKE

Kentmere
●
● Troutbeck

MILES
0 1 2 3 4

NATURAL FEATURES

The graceful cone of Ill Bell is a familiar object to most residents of south Westmorland and those visitors who approach Lakeland by way of Kendal and Windermere, although few who know it by sight can give it a name and fewer still its correct name. It is the dominating height on a steep-sided ridge, running north to High Street from the foothills of Garburn, and forms a most effective and imposing barrier between the Troutbeck and upper Kentmere valleys. It is linked by easy slopes to its neighbours, Yoke and Froswick, but both flanks are excessively steep: the Kentmere side in particular is very rough and the aspect of the fell from the upper reaches of the valley is magnificent. Crags descend northwards from the small summit. Ill Bell is distinctive and of good appearance, its peaked shape making it easily identifiable. The ridge on which it stands is probably the most popular fell-walk east of Kirkstone.

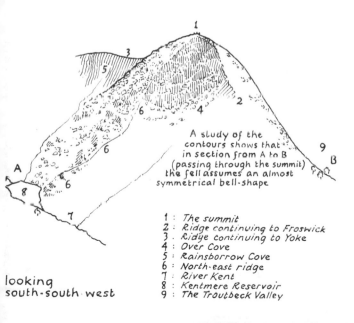

A study of the contours shows that in section from A to B (passing through the summit) the fell assumes an almost symmetrical bell-shape

1 : The summit
2 : Ridge continuing to Froswick
3 : Ridge continuing to Yoke
4 : Over Cove
5 : Rainsborrow Cove
6 : North-east ridge
7 : River Kent
8 : Kentmere Reservoir
9 : The Troutbeck Valley

looking
south-south west

MAP

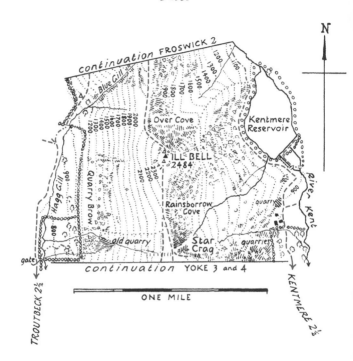

continuation FROSWICK 2

N

Blue Gill

Over Cove

Kentmere Reservoir

ILL BELL
2484

Hagg Gill

Quarry Brow

Rainsborrow Cove

River Kent

quarry

old quarry

Star Crag

quarries

gate

continuation YOKE 3 and 4

ONE MILE

TROUTBECK 2½

KENTMERE 2½

The Ill Bell ridge, from Stile End

ASCENT FROM GARBURN PASS
1050 feet of ascent : 2½ miles

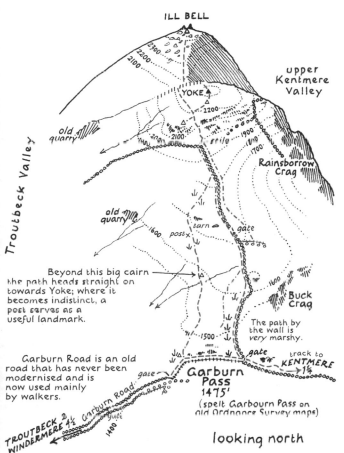

ILL BELL

2300
2200
2100

upper
Kentmere
Valley

YOKE

2200

old
quarry

2100
2000

1900

stile

1800

1700

Rainsborrow
Crag

Troutbeck Valley

old
quarry

1600

post ×

tarn

gate

1600

Buck
Crag

Beyond this big cairn
the path heads straight on
towards Yoke; where it
becomes indistinct, a
post serves as a
useful landmark.

1500

The path by
the wall is
very marshy.

Garburn Road is an old
road that has never been
modernised and is
now used mainly
by walkers.

gate

gate

Garburn
Pass
1475'

(spelt Garbourn Pass on
old Ordnance Survey maps)

track to
KENTMERE
1½

TROUTBECK 2
WINDERMERE 4½

Garburn Road

1400'

looking north

This is the obvious route to Ill Bell, and
the only easy one. As far as Yoke it is a dull walk
although the dreary foreground is relieved by the
splendid views to the west. The route throughout
is on grass, marshy in places, to the 1800' contour.

ASCENT FROM HAGG GILL, TROUTBECK
1700 feet of ascent

ASCENT FROM KENTMERE RESERVOIR
1500 feet of ascent

This is the *second* quarry in Hagg Gill (not the first). Turn right after the gate below the quarry, and then left, and left again (past a ruin). Carry on up the hill and ascend *beyond* the stream; a long featureless slope follows. *In mist, the quarry is dangerous when descending.*

looking north·east

Proceed to the head of the reservoir before turning up left to an obvious ridge. The rough upper slopes appear intimidating but steepness is the only difficulty. In wintry conditions this is a route for mountaineers only.

looking south·west

Ill Bell's continuously steep flanks are a challenge to those who prefer to reach their objective by rough scrambling, but walkers who walk for pleasure should take the easy promenade from the top of Garburn.

THE SUMMIT

The walker who toils up to the top of Ill Bell may be pardoned for feeling that he has achieved a major climb that has played a part of some consequence in mountaineering history, for he finds himself confronted by an imposing array of fine cairns that would do credit to a Matterhorn. And in fact this is a real mountain-top, small in extent and very rough; it is one of the most distinctive summits in Lakeland. Only one post remains of the wire fence that used to follow the ridge.

DESCENTS: The Troutbeck flank is steep, the Kentmere side is very steep and rough. Neither is suitable for descent, nor is there need to attempt them, for all destinations south are much more easily reached by way of the ridge to Garburn Pass.

In mist, Garburn Pass must be the objective. Join a path in the depression south of the summit and when it becomes indistinct keep on to a wall that continues to the Pass.

The main cairn

FROSWICK □ △ □ square cairn
post △ × viewpoint
broad cairn △ for Kentmere Reservoir
△ narrow cairn
GARBURN PASS   YOKE
2430   2300

N

50 YARDS

THE VIEW

Although higher fells northwards restrict the distant view in that direction, elsewhere it is good, the Scafells being prominent on the western skyline. Ill Bell is one of the classic 'stations' for viewing Windermere.

Principal Fells

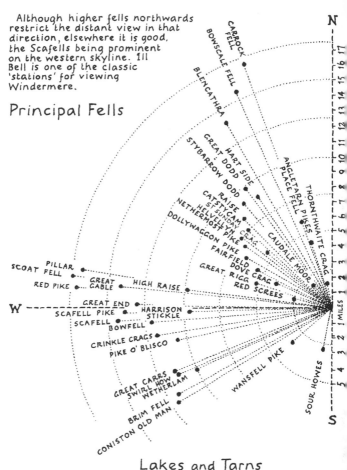

Lakes and Tarns

SSW : *Windermere*
SW : *Blelham Tarn*
NNW : A tiny strip of *Ullswater* is visible from the northern edge of the summit, 35 yards from main cairn.
E : *Kentmere Reservoir* is brought suddenly into view by walking 40 yards towards Harter Fell.

THE VIEW

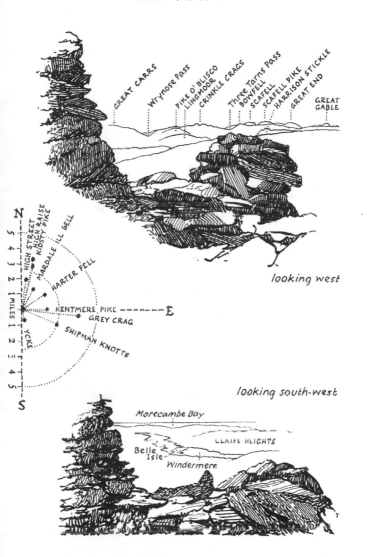

GREAT CARRS
Wrynose Pass
Pike o' Blisco
LINGMOOR
CRINKLE CRAGS
Three Tarns Pass
Bowfell
Scafell
Scafell Pike
HARRISON STICKLE
GREAT END
GREAT GABLE

looking west

N
5 4 3 2 1 MILES 1 2 3 4 5

HIGH STREET
KIDSTY PIKE
MARDALE ILL BELL
HARTER FELL
KENTMERE PIKE - - - - - E
GREY CRAG
SHIPMAN KNOTTS
YOKE

S

looking south-west

Morecambe Bay
CLAIFE HEIGHTS
Belle Isle
Windermere

Thornthwaite Crag
and Froswick

Two views
from the
summit

Rainsborrow Cove
and Yoke

RIDGE ROUTES

To FROSWICK, 2359' : ⅔ mile : NW then N
Depression at 2075' : 285 feet of ascent
Rough at first, then easy walking

Turn west by the most northerly
cairn, over stones (care needed
in mist), and find a path which
goes down north-west to the
depression, beyond which
is an easy climb on grass.

ONE MILE

To YOKE, 2316' : ⅔ mile : S
Depression at 2180' : 130 feet of ascent
An easy walk, safe in mist

Descend by the southerly cairn. A clear path
soon materialises and crosses the depression:
at the far end, where it bifurcates, take the
left branch along the edge of the escarpment.
There is nothing left of the wire fence that once
led to the cairn, except for a few fence posts, but
there is now a path all the way.

Ill Bell and the head of Kentmere

MARDALE HEAD

HIGH
STREET
HARTER FELL
ILL BELL
KENTMERE
PIKE ▲ TARN
CRAG
SHIPMAN KNOTTS

● Kentmere

Longsleddale ●

MILES
0   1   2   3   4

from Ill Bell
(north-east ridge)

NATURAL FEATURES

A high ridge, a counterpart to the Ill Bell range across Kentmere, rises steeply to enclose the upper part of that valley on the east. This is the south ridge of Harter Fell, which, soon after leaving the parent summit, swells into the bare, rounded top of Kentmere Pike, a fell of some importance and of more significance to the inhabitants of the valley, as its name suggests, than Harter Fell itself. The Kentmere slope, wooded at its foot and craggy above, is of little interest, but the eastern flank is altogether of sterner stuff, falling precipitously into the narrow jaws of Longsleddale: a most impressive scene. Here, abrupt cliffs riven by deep gullies tower high above the crystal waters of the winding Sprint and give to the dalehead a savageness that contrasts strikingly with the placid sweetness of the Sadgill pastures just out of their shadow.

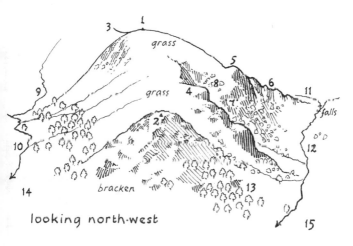

looking north-west

1: The summit	2: Shipman Knotts
3: Ridge continuing to Harter Fell	
4: Goat Scar	5: Steel Pike
6: Steel Rigg	7: Raven Crag
8: Settle Earth	9: Ullstone Gill
10: River Kent	11: Wren Gill
12: River Sprint	13: Sadgill Woods
14: Kentmere	15: Longsleddale

Steel Pike, from the quarry road

looking down a scree gully, eastern flank

MAP

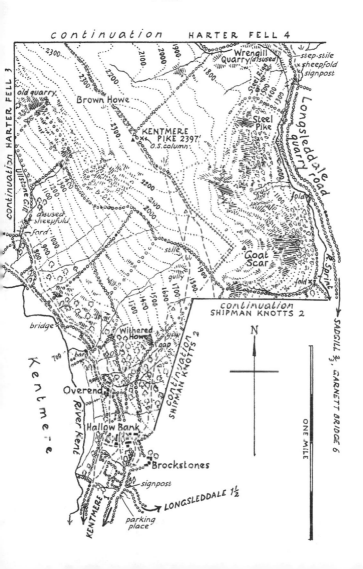

ASCENT FROM KENTMERE
1900 feet of ascent : 3 miles

KENTMERE PIKE
Ordnance Survey column
2300
2200
grass
2100
2000
scree
stile
1900
Goat Scar
1600
gully
1800
SHIPMAN KNOTTS
1500
grass
1700
gap
small walled enclosure (ruin)
Withered Howe
gap and post
gap
1400
1300
1200
bracken
groove
1100
boulder
1000
crag
ruins
gate
Hallow Bank
900
Brockstones
looking north
signpost
plantation
parking place
LONGSLEDDALE 1½ (cart track)
KENTMERE 1

This ascent of Kentmere Pike's tame western flank gives no suspicion of the rugged nature of the eastern face that falls precipitously to Longsleddale. A simple detour to the cairn above Goat Scar (a fine viewpoint for the craggy fastnesses of Longsleddale) is *very strongly* recommended in clear weather.

A gate to the right of the cluster of buildings at Hallow Bank gives access to the open fell. The path is indistinct initially, but it develops into a definite groove, easily followed to the first wall. There are three gaps in the wall, the correct one being marked by a post. In both ascent and descent it is necessary to turn right in order to avoid arriving at the wrong gap. There is a stile in the top wall which acts as a landmark.

The route shown is safe in mist.

A pleasant, well-graded climb along an old grooved path, with excellent views of Kentmere, although the last mile is dull. This is the easiest way onto the Harter Fell ridge.

ASCENT FROM LONGSLEDDALE
1850 feet of ascent : 3 miles from Sadgill

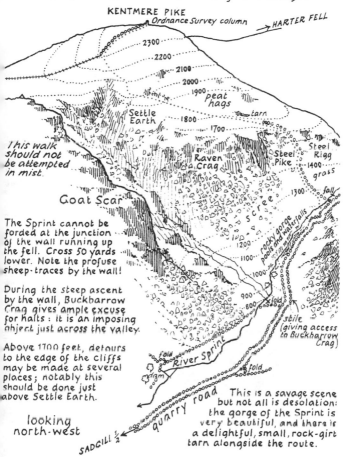

KENTMERE PIKE
Ordnance Survey column → HARTER FELL

2300
2200
2100
2000
1900 peat hags
tarn
Settle Earth
1800
1700
Raven Crag
Steel Pike
Steel Rigg
1400 grass

This walk should not be attempted in mist.

Goat Scar
scree
1300 fall
rock gorge pools and waterfalls
1200
1100
1000
900
800 fold
stile (giving access to Buckbarrow Crag)

The Sprint cannot be forded at the junction of the wall running up the fell. Cross 50 yards lower. Note the profuse sheep-traces by the wall!

During the steep ascent by the wall, Buckbarrow Crag gives ample excuse for halts : it is an imposing object just across the valley.

Above 1700 feet, detours to the edge of the cliffs may be made at several places ; notably this should be done just above Settle Earth.

fold
River Sprint
fold

looking north-west

SADGILL ½ ← quarry road

This is a savage scene but not all is desolation : the gorge of the Sprint is very beautiful, and there is a delightful, small, rock-girt tarn alongside the route.

This route has been devised for walkers who have a liking for impressive rock-scenery —— it is the only practicable way up the rough eastern face, and it affords striking views of the crags, first from below then in profile and lastly from above.

THE SUMMIT

The top of the fell, an unattractive and uninteresting place, is robbed of any appeal it might otherwise have had by a high wall that bisects it from end to end.   A triangulation station of the Ordnance Survey in the form of a short column stands in the shelter of the east side of the wall, on a small rise, but its claim to occupy the highest point is disputed by a cairn on the other side of the wall. The two are linked by a stile.

DESCENTS : To Kentmere : The middle section of the path down to Hallow Bank, between 1700 and 1300 feet, is difficult to follow. Anyone unfamiliar with the route should continue by the ridge over Shipman Knotts to the Sadgill-Kentmere cart-track: *in mist, this route is safest.*   For Longsleddale, too, it is best to make this cart-track the objective. *Much of the Longsleddale flank is craggy and dangerous,* although the route described as an ascent on page 6 is a safe way off in clear weather.

The eastern face, with Harter Fell beyond, from Goat Scar

THE VIEW

The distant view of Lakeland is interrupted by the nearer heights across Kentmere; it is interesting to note that the summit-cone of Ill Bell exactly conceals Scafell Pike. More satisfactory prospects are south-east, towards the Pennines, and south-west, over Windermere to Morecambe Bay.

Principal Fells

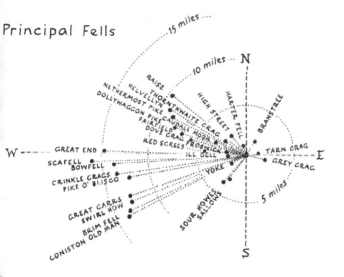

Lakes and Tarns

SSW : *Windermere*

Kentmere Reservoir is brought into view by walking 50 yards in the direction of Ill Bell.

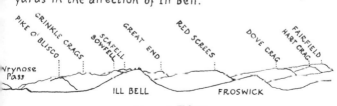

RIDGE ROUTES

To HARTER FELL, 2552': 1¼ miles
NNW then N

Depression at 2275': 275 feet of ascent
Easy walking on grass; safe in mist

Walls at first and then fences link the two summits (with traces of an earlier fence on the broad top of Harter Fell) and indicate the route; the path is intermittent.

HARTER FELL

2500

2400

The Knowe

2300

HALF A MILE

N

2200

Brown
Howe
peat hags

2300

x Ordnance Survey column
KENTMERE PIKE

KENTMERE PIKE
▲ Ordnance Survey column

2300

2200

N

HALF A MILE

2100

peat hags

2000

1900

Goat
Scar

1900

SHIPMAN
x KNOTTS

To SHIPMAN KNOTTS, 1926'
1¼ miles : SE then S

Depression at 1875': 80 feet of ascent
Easy walking, safe in mist

Continuous walls and fences link the summits but, in clear weather, a short detour (100 yards) should be made to the cairn on Goat Scar — an excellent viewpoint for Longsleddale. A scree gully and a steep crag distinguish the depression.

Branstree and the head of Longsleddale, from Goat Scar

Goat Scar
from
Longsleddale

Patterdale

Hartsop

▲ HIGH RAISE
RAMPSGILL HEAD
▲ KIDSTY PIKE

Riggindale
▲ HIGH STREET

MILES
0   1   2   3   4

from Twopenny Crag

NATURAL FEATURES

Travellers on the road and railway at Shap, looking west to the long undulating skyline of the High Street range, will find their attention focussing on the most prominent feature there, the sharp peak of Kidsty Pike. This distinctive summit, which unmistakably identifies the fell whenever it is seen in profile, is formed by the sudden breaking of the gently-rising eastern slope in a precipice of crags and scree that falls very abruptly into the depths of Riggindale. The summit is the best feature of the fell. The Riggindale face is everywhere steep, but other slopes are easy except for an extensive area of rock halfway down the long eastern shoulder.

It is interesting to note that the raising of the level of Haweswater gave Kidsty Pike a 'footing' on the shore of the lake, for the first time — previously the confining becks of Randale and Riggindale united before reaching the lake, but now each enters as a separate feeder and the small strip of shore between is the new terminus of the fell.

The summit crags

MAP

ONE MILE

ASCENT FROM MARDALE
1900 feet of ascent : 3 miles from the road end

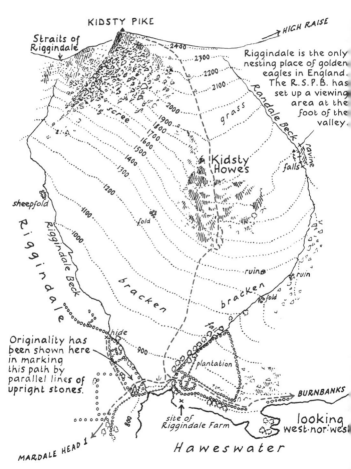

KIDSTY PIKE

→ HIGH RAISE

Straits of Rigindale

2400
2300
2200
2100
2000
1900
1800
1700
1600
1400
1300
1200
1100
1000
900
800

scree

grass

Riggindale Beck

ravine
falls

Kidsty Howes

Rigindale is the only nesting place of golden eagles in England. The R.S.P.B. has set up a viewing area at the foot of the valley.

sheepfold

Riggindale Beck

Riggindale

fold

bracken

ruin

ruin
fold

bracken

hide

Originality has been shown here in marking this path by parallel lines of upright stones.

plantation

BURNBANKS

looking west·nor·west

site of Riggindale Farm

MARDALE HEAD 1

Haweswater

The path over Kidsty Howes replaces an old route which made use of neglected and fading paths ascending to the right of the plantation. It is a much better approach. At the top of the steep ascent the path enters an interesting world of little rocky hills.

THE SUMMIT

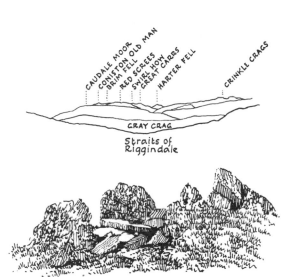

CAUDALE MOOR
CONISTON OLD MAN
BRIM FELL
RED SCREES
SWIRL HOW
GREAT CARRS
HARTER FELL
CRINKLE CRAGS

GRAY CRAG

Straits of
Riggindale

The summit is an eyrie perched high above Riggindale. The small cairn stands on grass amongst the boulders of the top pedestal, and crags are immediately below. The situation is dramatic. There is also a wind-shelter facing north-east.

DESCENTS. For Patterdale or Hartsop, make a bee-line over Rampsgill Head and join the path below The Knott. For Mardale use the path over Kidsty Howes. It starts just to the right of the wind-shelter. Obviously there is no direct way into Riggindale. *In mist*, keep to the Straits of Riggindale track if bound for Patterdale or Hartsop, the path for which is joined near a broken wall. For Mardale, follow the ridge to the east.

RIDGE ROUTE

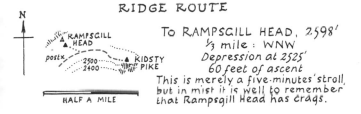

N

RAMPSGILL
HEAD

post x   2500   KIDSTY
          2400   PIKE

HALF A MILE

To RAMPSGILL HEAD, 2,598′
⅓ mile : WNW
Depression at 2525′
60 feet of ascent
This is merely a five-minutes' stroll, but in mist it is well to remember that Rampsgill Head has crags.

THE VIEW

The bulky masses of High Street,
Rampsgill Head and High Raise,
all in close proximity, cut out
big slices of the distant
panorama; but in those
directions where the view
is unrestricted, it is good.

Principal Fells

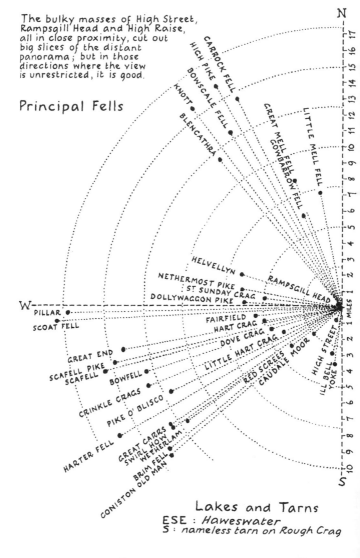

Lakes and Tarns
ESE : Haweswater
S : nameless tarn on Rough Crag

THE VIEW

High Street

Selside Pike and Haweswater

Compass bearings

N
5 4 3 2 1
HIGH RAISE
Low Raise
MILES
E
SELSIDE PIKE
BRANSTREE
TARN CRAG
HARTER FELL
S

The Knott

• Patterdale

Hartsop   ▲ HIGH RAISE
•
        ▲ ▲ RAMPSGILL HEAD
THE KNOTT

      ▲ HIGH STREET

MILES
0 1 2 3 4

from Hayeswater Gill

NATURAL FEATURES

The steep western slope descending from Rampsgill Head is arrested below the summit, just as the fall is gathering impetus, by a protuberance that takes the shape of a small conical hill. This is The Knott, a key point for walkers in this area, and although its short side rises barely a hundred feet from the main fell, its appearance is imposing when seen from other directions and especially when approached from the Hartsop valley. Fans of scree litter its western flank, which goes down steeply to Hayeswater; a tremendous scree gully here is The Knott's one interesting feature.

MAP

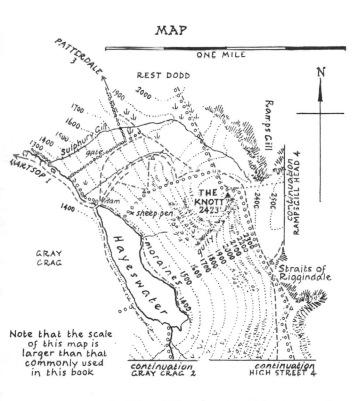

ONE MILE

N

PATTERDALE 3

REST DODD

1900
2000

1700
1600
1500
1400
1300

Sulphury Gill

gate

HARTSOP 1

Ramps Gill

CONTINUATION RAMPSGILL HEAD 4

1400

dam

sheep-pen

THE KNOTT 2423

2400
2300

GRAY CRAG

Hayeswater

moraines

gully

1500
1400

1900
1800
1700

2300
2200
2100
2000

Straits of Riggindale

Note that the scale of this map is larger than that commonly used in this book

continuation GRAY CRAG 2

continuation HIGH STREET 4

ASCENT FROM HARTSOP
1850 feet of ascent : 2 miles

THE KNOTT

HIGH STREET

REST DODD

2300
2200
2100 · scree
2000
1900
1800
1700

Scree gully

scree

peat-hags

PATTERDALE 3 ←

1700
1600
1500
1400
1300

gate

Sulphury Gill

Prison Gill

Sulphury Gill descends in a series of cascades

GRAY CRAG

sheep-pen

dam

Hayeswater

BROCK CRAGS

ford
cascades
1300
1200

gate
stile

filter house

gate — 1100
1000

1200
1100
1000
900
800
700

gate

Wath Bridge

barn

Pasture Beck

THRESHTHWAITE MOUTH

ruin
grid
ruins

Hayeswater Gill

The ford below the Hayeswater dam has outlived its usefulness — there is a footbridge further upstream.

Incidentally, this route is the quickest way to the High Street from the Kirkstone road

car park

Walker Bridge

Hartsop

looking east

As far as Hayeswater, this is a fine approach; beyond, it deteriorates into a dull trudge.

THE SUMMIT

HIGH RAISE   RAMPSGILL HEAD

The small top of the fell is without interest. A broken wall crosses the summit, forming an angle; a few paces away is the cairn.

DESCENTS : Follow the wall either way to join the path.

THE VIEW

Principal Fells

Eastwards the view is severely confined to the High Street range, but in other directions it is excellent

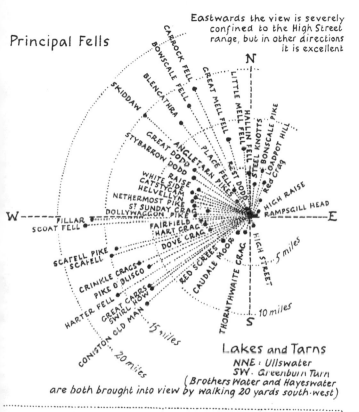

SKIDDAW
CARROCK FELL
BOWSCALE FELL
BLENCATHRA
GREAT MELL FELL
LITTLE MELL FELL
N
HALLIN FELL
STEEL KNOTTS
BONSCALE PIKE
LOADPOT HILL
Red Crag
GREAT DODD
ANGLETARN PIKES
STYBARROW DODD
PLACE FELL
REST DODD
WHITE SIDE
CATSTYCAM
HELVELLYN
NETHERMOST PIKE
ST SUNDAY CRAG
DOLLYWAGGON PIKE
HIGH RAISE
RAMPSGILL HEAD
W
PILLAR
SCOAT FELL
FAIRFIELD
HART CRAG
E
DOVE CRAG
SCAFELL PIKE
SCAFELL
RED SCREES
CRINKLE CRAGS
PIKE O'BLISCO
CAUDALE MOOR
THORNTHWAITE CRAG
HIGH STREET
5 miles
HARTER FELL
GREAT CARRS
SWIRL HOW
10 miles
S
15 miles
CONISTON OLD MAN
20 miles

Lakes and Tarns
NNE : Ullswater
SW : Greenburn Tarn
(Brothers Water and Hayeswater are both brought into view by walking 20 yards south-west)

RIDGE ROUTES

To RAMPSGILL HEAD, 2598' : ⅓ mile : E
Depression at 2360' : 225 feet of ascent
An easy climb. Avoid cliffs (on left) in mist

To REST DODD, 2283' : ¾ mile : NNW
Depression at 1925' : 360 feet of ascent
A straightforward walk, following the wall until it turns left, then directly ahead to the top

RAMPSGILL HEAD
2500
2400
THE KNOTT
2300
2100
2000
REST DODD
N
QUARTER MILE

from Sandwick

- • Pooley Bridge
- • Askham
- Helton •
- ▲ ARTHUR'S PIKE
- • Howtown
- LOADPOT
- ▲ HILL
- • Bampton
- ▲ WETHER HILL

MILES
0 1 2 3 4

The Beacon on The Pen

NATURAL FEATURES

The High Street range, narrow-waisted at the impressive Straits of Riggindale, thereafter develops buxom girth as it proceeds north. Although the western flank continues steep to its extremity on Arthur's Pike, the eastern slopes descend gradually and irresolutely, halting often in wide plateaux and covering a considerable tract of moorland that is intersected by a succession of deep-cut gills, all of which join the main lateral valley of Mardale and the River Lowther. Nowhere is this characteristic manifest more than in Loadpot Hill, and because Loadpot Hill is the last of the principal eminences of the range it also has northern slopes, no less extensive, which exhibit the same reluctance to depart from the high places. hence the gradients are easy, with subsidiary hillocks arresting the decline. By Lakeland standards (which demand at least a glimpse of *rock* in every scene) territory of this type is uninteresting, for all hereabouts is tough grass and heather except for the single shattered scree-rash of Brock Crag, above Fusedale; yet there is a haunting attractiveness about these far-flung rolling expanses. There is the appearance of desolation, but no place is desolate that harbours so much life: in addition to the inevitable sheep, hardy fell ponies roam and graze at will, summer and winter alike, and the Martindale deer often cross the watershed; in springtime especially, the number and variety of birds is quite unusual for the fells. There is little to disturb these creatures. Man is not the enemy, only the fox and the buzzard. Loadpot Hill is a natural sanctuary for all wild life.

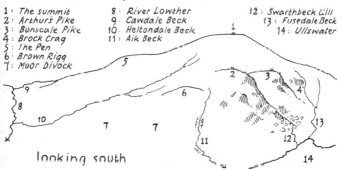

1 : The summit
2 : Arthur's Pike
3 : Bonscale Pike
4 : Brock Crag
5 : The Pen
6 : Brown Rigg
7 : Moor Divock

8 : River Lowther
9 : Cawdale Beck
10 : Heltondale Beck
11 : Aik Beck

12 : Swarthbeck Gill
13 : Fusedale Beck
14 : Ullswater

looking south

Cop Stone
and an oddly-sited
signpost

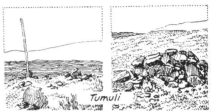

The antiquities
and oddities of
Moor Divock

Tumuli

Man may (and does) neglect Loadpot Hill nowadays, but it was not always so. There are evidences in plenty of the esteem with which it was regarded in the past. Even before the Romans traversed it with their High Street, its slopes were the home and meeting-place of man. Until recently there was a stone circle created by human agency near the headwaters of Swarthbeck Gill. There are Druidical remains and other curiosities in surprising profusion on Moor Divock on the 1050' contour, while,

A boundary stone

nearer our own time, men have laboured to erect an elaborate system of parochial boundary stones and posts along Loadpot's top and down its flanks. One of these, known as 'Lambert Lad', is unsquared and appears to be much older than the rest. And no other Lakeland fell has a concrete living-room floor and the remains of a domestic chimney-stack almost on its summit!

A boundary post

Moor Divock is of very special interest to the antiquarian and archæologist, and has long been a happy hunting-ground for them. The geologist will be concerned with investigating the crater-like hollows or sinkholes (locally known as swallows), which incidentally often contain carcasses and skeletons. The humbler pedestrian, not versed in the sciences, will be impressed by the spaciousness and loneliness of the scene and the excellence of its principal path.

Stone Circles

MAP

Loadpot Hill is the principal eminence of the High Street range at the northern extremity, and is extensive in area. Five pages of maps are necessary in order to show fully the main approaches to the fell from the villages at its base.

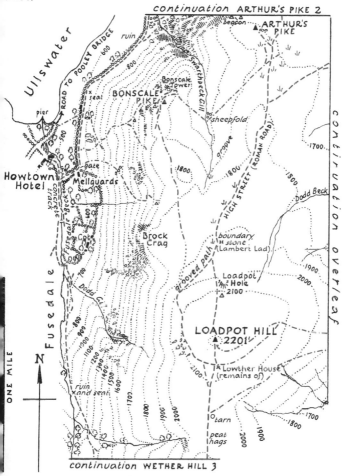

MAP

Reference should be made to the note at the top of page 8 before this map is consulted.

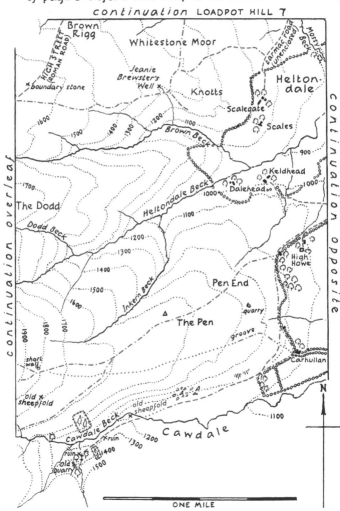

continuation LOADPOT HILL 7

ONE MILE

MAP

Reference should be made to the note at the top of page 8 before this map is consulted.

continuation LOADPOT HILL 8

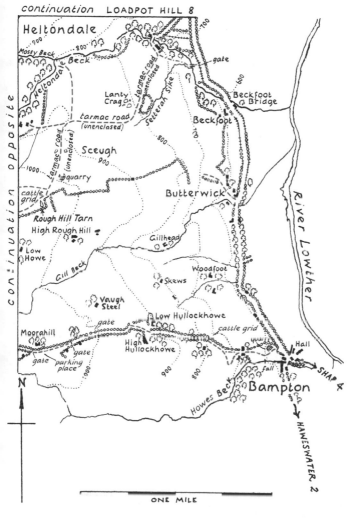

ONE MILE

MAP

Reference should be made to the note at the top of page 8 before this map is consulted.

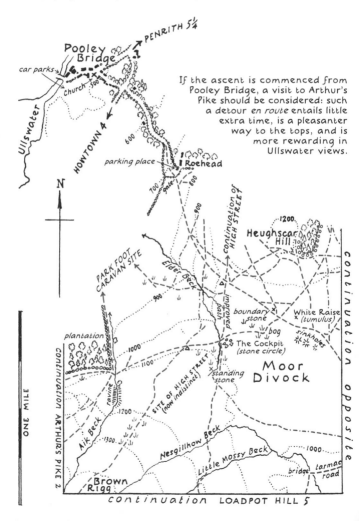

If the ascent is commenced from Pooley Bridge, a visit to Arthur's Pike should be considered: such a detour en *route* entails little extra time, is a pleasanter way to the tops, and is more rewarding in Ullswater views.

MAP

NOTE on the Loadpot Hill maps:

Walkers bound for the summit, especially from the north and east, may have difficulty in finding access to the fell: routes cannot be determined by observation from valley-level because of intervening tracts of cultivated farmland, which must be traversed before open ground is reached. A maze of byways and walled enclosures and farmsteads complicates the approaches. Many variations may be made, but the accompanying maps illustrate only the most direct routes, and, to depict them more clearly, *much unnecessary detail in the cultivated areas has been omitted.*

Those walkers who, like the author, do not enjoy encounters with cows and young bulls and the sundry other mammals that commonly frequent confined farmyards will be relieved to learn that the routes illustrated have been specially selected to reduce this possibility to a minimum. At one place (Carhullan) it is necessary to pass through a farmyard, but it is no longer a working farm.

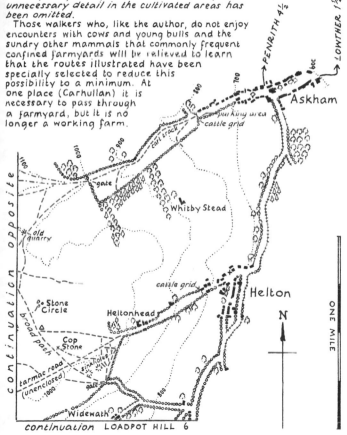

ASCENTS FROM BAMPTON AND HELTON
1650 feet of ascent
4½ miles from Bampton ; 5½ miles from Helton

Black fell ponies graze on the upper slopes They are docile

There is one breach in the cultivated land where the moor comes down almost to the road: the Helton route traverses this

looking west

The first field on the approach from Bampton —a common— has many charming waterfalls, and more rock than will be met on the whole of the rest of the walk

The Helton route is rather the more interesting of the two illustrated, but both are pleasant walks in quiet, unexciting surroundings. The upper slopes are simple and very easy, but deceptively long.

ASCENT FROM MOOR DIVOCK
1300 feet of ascent : 4½ miles

Full route from POOLEY BRIDGE
1800 feet of ascent : 6 miles

Full route from ASKHAM
1600 feet of ascent : 6½ miles

Fell ponies are likely to
be seen on these slopes
where they live all the year.
When the fell is under deep snow
they are fed from the farms.
Many used to work in the coal-pits.

The gradients are
everywhere simple.
Even the most
decrepit hiker
will surmount
them with ease.

LOADPOT HILL

remains of
Lowther
House

grass

2100

Loadpot
Hole

2000

grass

groove

boundary
stone ✕

1900

rutted path

HIGH STREET
(ROMAN ROAD)

Swarthbeck Gill

sheepfold

1800

1700

beacon

ARTHUR'S
PIKE

✕ boundary
stone

grass

1600

Jeanie Brewster's
Well is not easily
found.

✕ Jeanie
Brewster's
Well

1500

1400

1300

1000

gorse

1200

1100

Brown
Rigg

heather

White
Knott

Heltondale

bridge

tarmac road
(unfenced)

HELTON

signpost
Cop
Stone✕

heather

Stone
Circle

Stone
Circle

WIDE PATH

Wolf
Holes

sinkholes

Pulpit
Holes

ravine

bracken

HOWTOWN

Aik Beck

1100

Moor
Divock

tumulus

boundary
stone

bog

Stone
Circle

Elder Beck

ASKHAM

bracken

bracken

good wide path

POOLEY BRIDGE

looking south-south-west

Bridge in Heltondale

This is not a walk for a wet or misty day, and ample
time should be allowed. The High Street of the Romans is
now, at best, only a line of ruts in the grass. The ascent
via Arthur's Pike is recommended for its superior views.

ASCENT FROM HOWTOWN
1750 feet of ascent : 2¼ miles

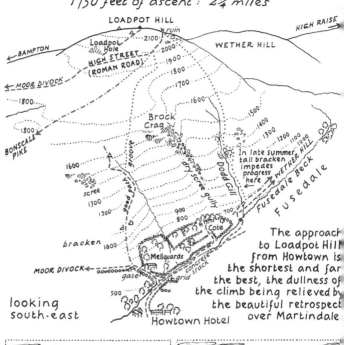

LOADPOT HILL

HIGH RAISE

← BAMPTON

Loadpot Hole

×ruin

2100

2000

WETHER HILL

HIGH STREET
(ROMAN ROAD)

1900

← MOOR DIVOCK

1800

1700

1800

1600

1800

1500

1400

Brock Crag

1300

1200

1100

1000

BONSCALE PIKE

1300

In late summer tall bracken impedes progress here

WETHER HILL

1600

groove

dry scree gully

Dodd Gill

Fusedale Beck

FUSEDALE

scree

1300

1200

1300

900

800

700

Cote

bracken

1000

Meliguards

MOOR DIVOCK ←

gate

concrete track

grid

500

looking
south-east

Howtown Hotel

The approach to Loadpot Hill from Howtown is the shortest and far the best, the dullness of the climb being relieved by the beautiful retrospect over Martindale

Fusedale and Ullswater from Dodd Gill

Brock Crag and Ullswater

THE SUMMIT

Reference has already been made to the attention paid to Loadpot Hill since ancient times, and this is also manifest in the cairn on the summit — somebody, sometime, has gone to the trouble to collect, somewhere, a number of handsome stones foreign to the immediate neighbourhood, all prominently displaying a glittering quartz content, and transport them, somehow, to the highest point; at one time these formed a cairn around the base of a boundary stone, as in the illustration, but now this stone lies on top of the cairn and some of the quartz stones have been dispersed.

Apart from this cairn, and a triangulation column (no. 10789), the summit is unremarkable. All is grass and all is flat, and more like a 30-acre field than a mountain top.

DESCENTS : Descents may be made easily and safely in any direction. (Loadpot *Hole* is not a hazard to avoid — it is not a hole one can fall into but a shallow landslip, which, because it faces north, holds the last snow on the fell every spring.)

In mist, the walker should not be here at all, but if he is his best plan is probably to descend northwards to the High Street (only a rut in the grass) and follow it to Moor Divock. *If conditions are bad*, go west, crossing the High Street, down the steepening bracken slopes into Fusedale (for Howtown).

Just below and south of the summit are the remains of Lowther House, formerly a shooting lodge. Fifty years ago its stone chimney stack was still to be seen pointing forlornly at the sky — a landmark that distinguished this fell from all others. Today, all that is left is part of the concrete floor and a pile of stones.

Chimney of Lowther House (now fallen)

THE VIEW

Principal Fells

One half of the panorama is Lakeland, dominated by the high, imposing range of Helvellyn; the other half is Pennine, with Cross Fell and its satellites prominent

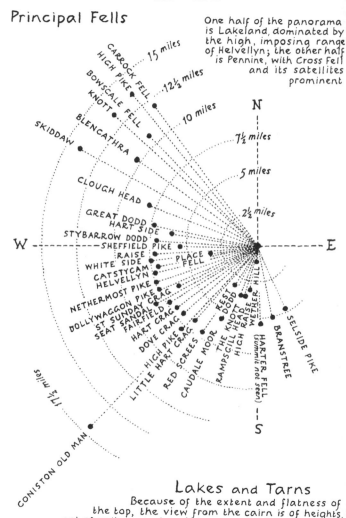

Lakes and Tarns

Because of the extent and flatness of the top, the view from the cairn is of heights, not of valleys, and no lakes are visible. Ullswater, however, can be seen by walking 150 yards towards the west

RIDGE ROUTES

TO ARTHUR'S PIKE, 1747': 2¼ miles
NW, then NNE and N
Minor depressions: 50 feet of ascent
An easy walk, not recommended in mist

Follow the path north until
it joins the High Street,
and keep straight on for
about a mile. Then bear
left for the summit.
Visit the beacon for the
best view of Ullswater.

TO BONSCALE PIKE, 1718'
1½ miles: NW, then N
Minor depressions:
50 feet of ascent
An easy walk, not safe in mist

Descend the easy western slope
to the High Street, but at the
angle of the path leave it
and continue north over
sundry grassy mounds (faint
path) to the inconspicuous
cairn above a fringe of crag
where stand two prominent
pillars, the lower of the two
being Bonscale Tower.

TO WETHER HILL, 2210'
1 mile: S
Depression at 2025'
200 feet of ascent
An easy walk, safe in mist

The High Street inclined to the left
below Lowther House, but has become
indistinct and is now badly cut about
by peat-hags in the depression. Easier
walking is found on the path, quite easy
to follow, which crosses the depression
on its right (i.e. west) side, away from
the hags. There should be no difficulty
in mist: all gradients are easy — if
steep ground is encountered
the route is lost.

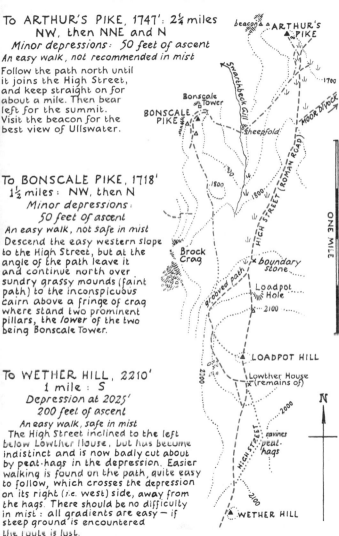

HIGH STREET
▲

Mardale
● Head

▲
MARDALE
ILL BELL

▲ HARTER FELL

▲ ILL BELL

● Kentmere

MILES
0 1 2 3 4

from the north ridge of
Branstree

NATURAL FEATURES

Mardale Ill Bell has received scant mention in Lakeland literature, and admittedly is mainly of nondescript appearance, yet one aspect of the fell is particularly good and appeals on sight to all who aspire to a little mild mountaineering. This is to the north-east, where a boulder-strewn shoulder leaves the summit and soon divides into two craggy ridges, enclosing a rocky corrie; the rugged surroundings on this side are greatly enhanced in impressiveness by the two splendid tarns of Blea Water (below High Street) and Small Water (below Harter Fell), each of them occupying a volcanic crater and deeply inurned amongst crags. These tarns, with their streams, are collectively known as Mardale Waters, and greatly contribute to the fine scenic quality of this typical Lakeland landscape.

To the west the fell merges gently and dully into High Street, with a fringe of crag throughout on the north; and south of the linking high ground is a wall of steep rock, Bleathwaite Crag, bounding the silent hollow of Hall Cove, the birthplace of the River Kent. On the south also is the most pronounced shoulder of the fell, Lingmell End, thrusting far into the valley of Kentmere, and from it descends a short spur to the top of Nan Bield Pass.

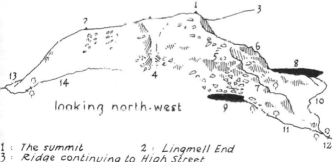

looking north-west

1 : The summit   2 : Lingmell End
3 : Ridge continuing to High Street
4 : Nan Bield Pass   5 : Piot Crag   6 : North ridge
7 : East ridge   8 : Blea Water   9 : Small Water
10 : Blea Water Beck   11 : Small Water Beck
12 : Dodderwick Force   13 : River Kent   14 : Lingmell Gill

Waterfalls,
River Kent
below Hall Cove

Dodderwick
Force

The north face
from Blea Water

MAP

ASCENT FROM MARDALE
1700 feet of ascent : 2 miles from the road end

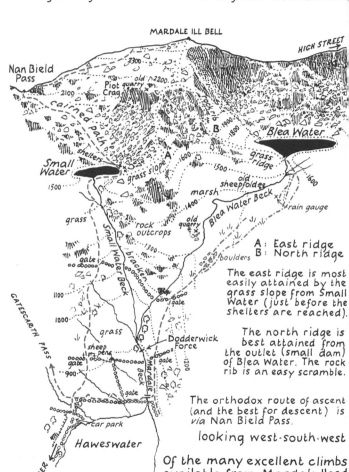

MARDALE ILL BELL

HIGH STREET

Nan Bield Pass

2300

old 2200 quarry

Piot Crag

2100

cairned path

shelter

Small Water

1500

grass slope

B

1800

Blea Water

1900

grass ridge

A

1600

1500

old sheepfolds

marsh

1600

1400

Blea Water Beck

rain gauge

grass

rock outcrops

old quarry

1300

boulders

Small Water Beck

gate

1100

bracken

1000

grass

sheep pens

gate

900

Dodderwick Force

gate

Mardale Beck

1200

gate

GATESCARTH PASS

car park

Haweswater

HAWESWATER HOTEL 2½

A: East ridge
B: North ridge

The east ridge is most
easily attained by the
grass slope from Small
Water (just before the
shelters are reached).

The north ridge is
best attained from
the outlet (small dam)
of Blea Water. The rock
rib is an easy scramble.

The orthodox route of ascent
(and the best for descent) is
via Nan Bield Pass.

looking west·south·west

Of the many excellent climbs
available from Mardale Head
the direct ascent of Mardale Ill Bell ranks
high, the walk being favoured by striking views
of two of the finest tarns in Lakeland, each set
amongst crags in wild and romantic surroundings.

ASCENT FROM KENTMERE
2100 feet of ascent : 4¾ miles

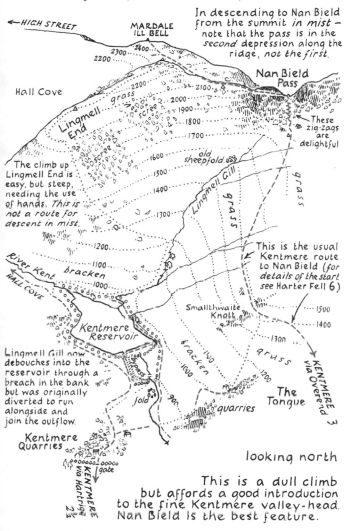

In descending to Nan Bield from the summit *in mist* — note that the pass is in the *second* depression along the ridge, not the *first*.

←HIGH STREET

MARDALE
ILL BELL

Nan Bield
Pass

Hall Cove

2400
2300
2200

2200
grass
scree
2100
2000
1900
1800
1700

Lingmell End

These zig-zags are delightful

The climb up Lingmell End is easy, but steep, needing the use of hands. *This is not a route for descent in mist.*

scree

old sheepfold

1600
1500
1400
1300

Lingmell Gill

grass

grass

River Kent

HALL COVE

1200
1100
bracken
1000

This is the usual Kentmere route to Nan Bield *(for details of the start see Harter Fell 6)*

Smallthwaite Knott

1500
1400
1300

Kentmere Reservoir

grass

KENTMERE via Overend 3

Lingmell Gill now debouches into the reservoir through a breach in the bank but was originally diverted to run alongside and join the outflow.

bracken

1100
1000

fold

The Tonque

Kentmere Quarries

quarries

KENTMERE via Hartrigg 2½

gate

looking north

This is a dull climb but affords a good introduction to the fine Kentmere valley-head. Nan Bield is the best feature.

THE SUMMIT

Haweswater

Haweswater

A large cairn, more shapely than the one illustrated, crowns the undulating top, which is characterised by soft turf, patches of brown stones and occasional outcrops. There is nothing here to suggest the presence of fine crags close by, and a visit to them (north) adds interest to the summit.

DESCENTS: The usual way off is via Nan Bield Pass (the wall-shelter on the top of the pass is plainly visible from the summit-cairn); to reach it, keep to the right of the direct line until a cairned path materialises. Both the north and east ridges are rough and the Lingmell End route is steep.

In mist, aim for Nan Bield Pass, noting that it crosses the second depression reached, not the first.

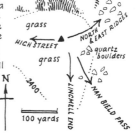

grass

NORTH & EAST RIDGES

HIGH STREET

grass

quartz boulders

2400

LINGMELL END

NAN BIELD PASS

N

100 yards

The stone shelters at Small Water

THE VIEW

Outstanding in the moderate view is the neighbouring ridge of Ill Bell, which, displaying its steep and rugged eastern face, looks magnificent from this angle. The long curve of High Street hides most of the western fells, and only the tips of the Bowfell group are visible above the rising skyline of Thornthwaite Crag.

Principal Fells

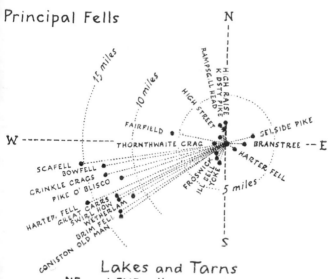

Lakes and Tarns

NE and ENE : Haweswater (two sections)

Neither *Blea Water* nor *Small Water* can be seen from the cairn but both are worth the detour necessary to obtain bird's-eye views of them, the former from a break in the crags 100 yards north, the latter from above Piot Crag a quarter of a mile due east.

The stone shelters at Small Water (illustration opposite)

Testimony to the former importance of Nan Bield Pass as a route for travellers and trade are the three shelters alongside the track where it crosses the bouldery shore of Small Water — erected for wayfarers overtaken by bad weather or darkness. These shelters are roughly but soundly built and roofed, but they are low and can be entered only by crawling. Once the body is insinuated snugly in their spider-infested recesses, however, the weather may be defied.

RIDGE ROUTES

To HIGH STREET, 2718': $\frac{4}{5}$ mile : WNW then NW
Depression at 2350': 400 feet of ascent
An easy walk with interesting views

There is a path from the summit to the broken wall, but it is preferable to follow the edge of the escarpment after crossing the depression. At one point, marked 'A', there is a sensational downward view of Blea Water. In mist, keep to the path.

To THORNTHWAITE CRAG, 2569'
$1\frac{1}{3}$ miles : WNW, then WSW, W & NW
Depressions at 2350' and 2475'
250 feet of ascent
Easy walking, confusing in mist

Cut across to the west to join the path coming up from Nan Bield. When this bends left keep straight on along a fainter path to the wall corner. From there a path cuts across to Thornthwaite Crag.

HIGH STREET
Ordnance Survey column
Blea Water
THORNTHWAITE CRAG
MARDALE ILL BELL
ONE MILE

To HARTER FELL, 2552': 1 mile : SE, then ESE and E
Depression at 2100' (Nan Bield Pass) : 500 feet of ascent
A rough but interesting walk, with beautiful and impressive views

Aim first for the top of Nan Bield Pass (the wall-shelter there is in view from the summit), keeping to the right of the direct line until a cairned path to it is reached. Beyond the pass, an interesting ridge rises in rocky steps to the flat top of Harter Fell.   In mist, the main difficulty will be in locating the Pass

MARDALE ILL BELL
quartz boulders
MARDALE
Nan Bield Pass
Small Water Crag
HALF A MILE
HARTER FELL
KENTMERE

Haweswater and Small Water
from the Nan Bield ridge.

The summit crags

from Rampsgill Beck

Howtown ●
● Martindale
BEDA FELL ▲
WETHER ▲ HILL
● Patterdale
▲ THE NAB
REST DODD ▲
▲ HIGH RAISE

MILES

0   1   2   3   4

The Nab is situated wholly within the Martindale Deer Forest. The boundaries of the Forest are principally defined by the 'Forest Wall' which encloses much of the Ramps Gill and Bannerdale valleys and crosses the high ground between. This wall does not confine the deer — they roam freely beyond the boundaries — but it marks their home, their only safe refuge, their one sanctuary.
  PLEASE DO NOT INTRUDE.

Red Deer Stag

NATURAL FEATURES

The Nab is, in character, akin to the three Dodds around Kirkstonefoot. Very steep-sided, soaring in symmetrical lines to a slender cone, it appears from the pastures of Martindale as a lofty wedge splitting the valley into two branches, Ramps Gill and Bannerdale: from this viewpoint it may well be thought to be a separate and solitary fell. But in fact, as is seen from neighbouring heights, it is merely the butt of the northern shoulder of Rest Dodd. Its lower slopes are of bracken, its higher reaches of grass, with occasional scree on both flanks and a few rocks on Nab End. In addition to its other distinctions it has, on the wide ridge behind the summit, a most unpleasant morass of peat-hags, one of the worst in the district.

MAP

Martindale Deer Forest is home to the oldest herd of native red deer in England. Walkers are asked to keep to the preferred routes described on page 3, and to avoid disturbing the deer.

to MARTINDALE CHURCH 1¼

Dale Head

The Bungalow

Bannerdale

Bannerdale Beck

ROAD

PRIVATE ROAD

gully

hurdle

Nab End

THE NAB 1887

N

Yewgrove Gill

falls

Ramps Gill

Rampsgill Beck

ONE MILE

continuation REST DODD 2

ASCENTS

The 'Keep Out' notices, barricaded gates and miles of barbed wire have gone from The Nab and most of the fell is now public access land. However, it is a red deer conservation area and wandering within the boundaries of the Deer Forest is not encouraged. Some fifty years ago, the author carried out his explorations surreptitiously, and without permission (not caring to risk a refusal); he was not detected, but this may possibly have been due to his marked resemblance to an old stag, and others should not expect the same good fortune.

To limit disturbance to the herd, walkers today are asked to keep to the preferred routes described below, to pay attention to local signs, and to keep away from the deer at calving time in June and July. Between September and February the area may sometimes be closed for deer management—for further information, contact the Dalemain Estate Office (tel. 017684 86450).

In general, walkers are requested to follow the informal agreement to approach the summit only by way of the ridge from Rest Dodd (see page 2) and to return the same way.

The preferred route of ascent from Martindale is from Dale Head Farm, where walkers should follow the Patterdale path which goes through the wicket gate below the farmhouse onto the fell. The path follows the boundary wall of the fields, slowly climbing towards Angle Tarn (see Angletarn Pikes 6). On coming within sight of the tarn, swing east behind Buck Crag to the gate at Satura Crag and then onto Rest Dodd and The Nab (see Rest Dodd 6, top and bottom).

Alternatively, the longer ascent is from Martindale Old Church, climbing on the east side of the valley above Gowk Hill onto High Raise (see High Raise 6) and then around the head of the valley to The Knott and on to Rest Dodd as before.

THE SUMMIT

The summit, a shapely dome, is completely grassy. A few stones have been carried up and make an untidy cairn.

THE VIEW

Principal Fells

The view is 'open' only to the north. The most interesting feature, however, is the snug fit of Scafell Pike in the frame of Deepdale Hause

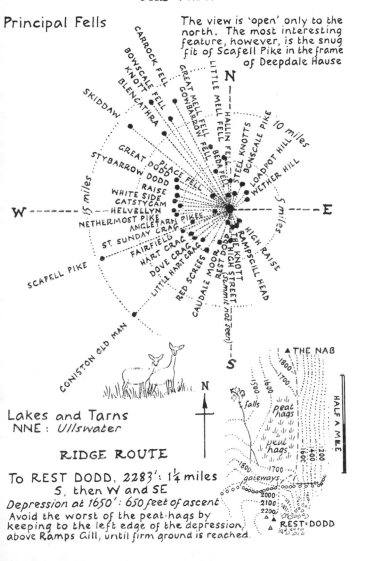

CARROCK FELL
BOWSCALE FELL
KNOTT
BLENCATHRA
SKIDDAW
GREAT MELL FELL
GOWBARROW FELL
LITTLE MELL FELL
N
HALLIN FELL
STEEL KNOTTS
BONSCALE PIKE
10 miles
LOADPOT HILL
WETHER HILL
GREAT DODD
STYBARROW DODD
PLACE FELL
BEDA FELL
RAISE
WHITE SIDE
CATSTYCAM
HELVELLYN
NETHERMOST PIKE
ANGLETARN PIKES
15 miles
5 miles
W
E
ST. SUNDAY CRAG
FAIRFIELD
HART CRAG
DOVE CRAG
LITTLE HART CRAG
RED SCREES
CAUDALE MOOR
REST DODD
HIGH STREET (summit not seen)
THE KNOTT
RAMPSGILL HEAD
HIGH RAISE
SCAFELL PIKE
S
CONISTON OLD MAN

Lakes and Tarns
NNE: *Ullswater*

N

RIDGE ROUTE

To REST DODD, 2283': 1¼ miles
S, then W and SE
Depression at 1650': 650 feet of ascent
Avoid the worst of the peat-hags by keeping to the left edge of the depression, above Ramps Gill, until firm ground is reached.

▲ THE NAB

HALF A MILE

1800
1700
1600
1500
falls
peat hags
1200
1400
1600
peat hags
1800
1700
gateways
2000
2100
2200
△ REST DODD

Place Fell

2154'

from Birks

Howtown •

▲ PLACE FELL

• Patterdale

MILES

0   1   2   3

Few fells are so well favoured as Place Fell for appraising neighbouring heights.   It occupies an exceptionally good position in the curve of Ullswater, in the centre of a great bowl of hills; its summit commands a very beautiful and impressive panorama. On a first visit to Patterdale, Place Fell should be an early objective, for no other viewpoint gives such an appreciation of the design of this lovely corner of Lakeland.

NATURAL FEATURES

Place Fell rises steeply from the curve formed by the upper and middle reaches of Ullswater and its bulky mass dominates the head of the lake. Of only moderate elevation, and considerably overtopped by surrounding heights, nevertheless the fell more than holds its own even in such a goodly company: it has that distinctive blend of outline and rugged solidity characteristic of the true mountain. Many discoveries await those who explore: in particular the abrupt western flank, richly clothed with juniper and bracken and heather, and plunging down to the lake in a rough tumble of crag and scree, boulders and birches, is a paradise for the scrambler, while a more adventurous walker will find a keen enjoyment in tracing the many forgotten and overgrown paths across the fellside and in following the exciting and airy sheep-tracks that so skilfully contour the steep upper slopes below the hoary crest.

The eastern face, overlooking Boredale, is riven by deepcut gullies and is everywhere steep. Northward two ridges descend more gradually to the shores of Ullswater after passing over minor summits; from a lonely hollow between them issues the main stream on the fell, Scalehow Beck, which has good waterfalls. To the south, Boredale Hause is a well-known walkers' crossroads, and beyond this depression high ground continues to climb towards the principal watershed.

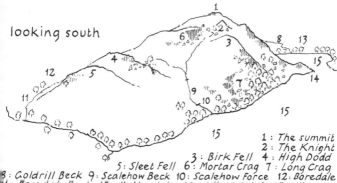

looking south

1 : The summit
2 : The Knight
3 : Birk Fell   4 : High Dodd
5 : Sleet Fell 6 : Mortar Crag 7 : Long Crag
8 : Goldrill Beck 9 : Scalehow Beck 10 : Scalehow Force 12 : Boredale
11 : Boredale Beck 13 : Patterdale 14 : Silver Point 15 : Ullswater

MAP

It is the author's opinion that the lakeside path from Scalehow Beck, near Sandwick, to Patterdale (in that direction) is the most beautiful and rewarding walk in Lakeland.
The junction of paths at Silver Bay is marked by a large cairn.

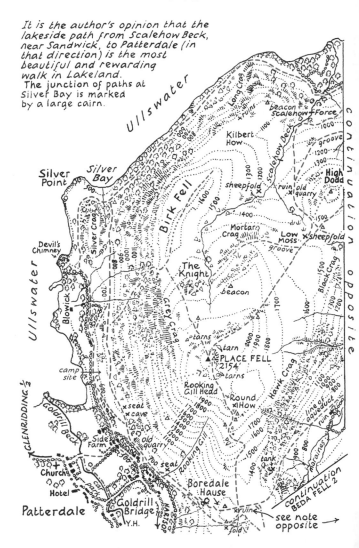

MAP

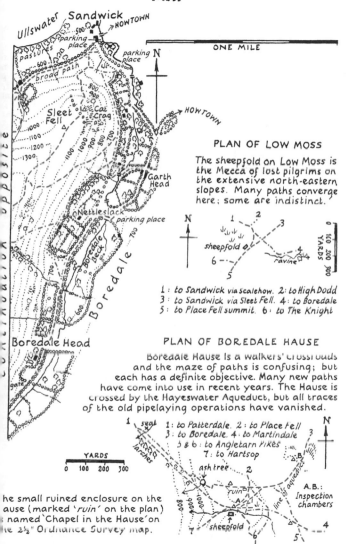

ONE MILE

Ullswater Sandwick → HOWTOWN
pastures
500
parking place
600
broad path
parking place N
→ HOWTOWN
Sleet Fell
Cat Crag
1000
1100
1200
1300
Garth Head
Nettleslack
parking place
700
Boredale Beck
Boredale
700
700
600
Boredale Head
gate

Continuation opposite

PLAN OF LOW MOSS

The sheepfold on Low Moss is the Mecca of lost pilgrims on the extensive north-eastern slopes. Many paths converge here; some are indistinct.

N

1   2
3
sheepfold
4
6
ravine
5

0 100 200 300 YARDS

1 : to Sandwick via Scalehow. 2 : to High Dodd.
3 : to Sandwick via Sleet Fell. 4 : to Boredale.
5 : to Place Fell summit. 6 : to The Knight.

PLAN OF BOREDALE HAUSE

Boredale Hause is a walkers' crossroads and the maze of paths is confusing; but each has a definite objective. Many new paths have come into use in recent years. The Hause is crossed by the Hayeswater Aqueduct, but all traces of the old pipelaying operations have vanished.

1 seat
larches
N

1 : to Patterdale. 2 : to Place Fell.
3 : to Boredale. 4 : to Martindale.
5 & 6 : to Angletarn Pikes.
7 : to Hartsop
3
B
ash tree
2
line of aqueduct
800
ruin
A
A.B. : Inspection chambers
7
sheepfold
6
5
4

YARDS
0 100 200 300

he small ruined enclosure on the
ause (marked 'ruin' on the plan)
named 'Chapel in the Hause' on
he 2½" Ordnance Survey map.

ASCENT FROM PATTERDALE
1700 feet of ascent : 1¾ miles

The face of Place Fell overlooking Patterdale is unremittingly and uncompromisingly steep, and the ascent is invariably made by way of the easier gradients of Boredale Hause, there being a continuous path on this route. (*From the valley there appear to be paths going straight up the fell, but these are not paths at all: they are incipient streams and runnels.*) As an alternative an old neglected track that branches from the higher path to Silver Bay is recommended: this slants leftwards to the skyline depression between Birk Fell and Grey Crag. This old track is difficult to locate from above and is better not used for descent as there is rough ground in the vicinity.

looking
north-north-east

The diversion of the old track from the higher path to Silver Bay occurs a full half-mile beyond the quarry at a point where there is a bluff of grey rock on the left above some larches. A flat boulder marks the junction, and a few ancient cairns along the route are also a help. Botanists will find much of interest here.
Some 200 yards up the old track there was once a faint path turning away on the right: it climbed high across the face below Grey Crag, vanishing on scree only to reappear beyond, on the 1500' contour and continuing all the way to the usual route *via* Boredale Hause. This path has disappeared altogether but the route may still be attempted. It makes an exhilarating high-level walk.
On the Boredale Hause route, take the upper path at the fork near the seat. Watch for the zig-zag: if this is missed the walker naturally gravitates to the lower path. The striking ash tree is on the *upper* path.

One cannot sojourn at Patterdale without looking at Place Fell and one cannot look long at Place Fell without dully setting forth to climb it. The time is very well spent.

ASCENT FROM SANDWICK
1700 feet of ascent : 2½ miles

Of the two routes shown from Low Moss to the summit, the one on the left is *very much* the better.

PLACE FELL

Top of Grey Crag

The Knight

grass
beacon
groove
Mortar Crag
Low Moss
sheepfold
grass
Birk Fell
ravine
High Dodd
ruin
sheepfold
BOREDALE HAUSE
← path choked with bracken in summer
groove
barn
Sleet Fell
old wall
← path starts 170 yards past double bend in wall
Nettleslack
barn
Boredale Beck
bracken
groove
Scalehow Beck
beacon
Scalehow Force
PATTERDALE 3
barn
seat
broad path
Ullswater
HOWTOWN 1½
parking place
Sandwick Beck
ROAD
signpost
parking place
HOWTOWN 1¼
Sandwick

looking south-west

Five alternatives are shown for the initial part of the climb, the best on a clear day being over the top of Sleet Fell (which is steep). All ways converge near the sheepfold on Low Moss, beyond which is a further choice.

THE SUMMIT

A rocky ridge overtops gently-rising slopes and has a cairn at one end and a triangulation column at the other. There is a better cairn farther north.

DESCENTS : Routes of descent are indicated in the illustration of the view; that to Boredale Hause is safest in bad weather.

Place Fell 7

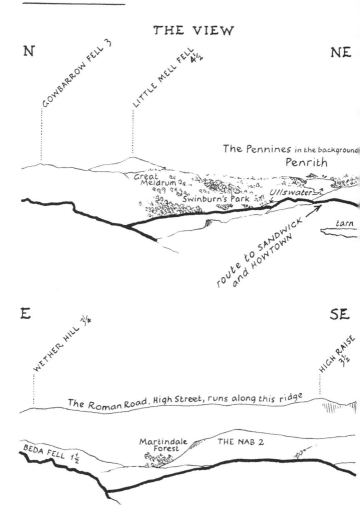

THE VIEW

N   NE

COWBARROW FELL 3

LITTLE MELL FELL 4½

The Pennines in the background
Penrith

Great Meldrum

Swinburn's Park

Ullswater

route to SANDWICK and HOWTOWN

tarn

E   SE

WETHER HILL ¾

HIGH RAISE 3½

The Roman Road, High Street, runs along this ridge

BEDA FELL 1½

Martindale Forest

THE NAB 2

The thick line marks the visible boundaries
of Place Fell from the summit cairn.
The figures following the names of fells
indicate distances in miles.

THE VIEW

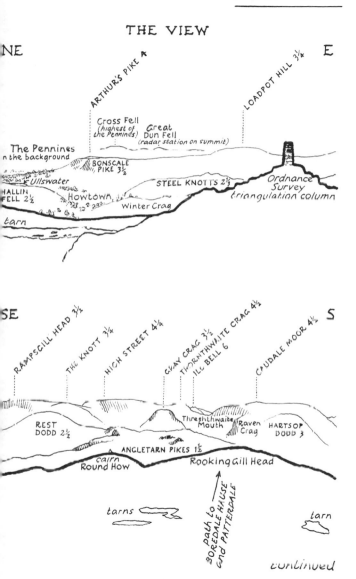

NE

ARTHUR'S PIKE ▲

LOADPOT HILL ¾★ E

Cross Fell
(highest of
the Pennines)

Great
Dun Fell
(radar station on summit)

The Pennines
in the background

BONSCALE
PIKE 3½

STEEL KNOTTS 2⅓

Ullswater

HALLIN
FELL 2½

Howtown

Winter Crag

Ordnance
Survey
triangulation column

tarn

SE

RAMPSGILL HEAD 3½

THE KNOTT ¾

HIGH STREET 4¼

GRAY CRAG 3½

THORNTHWAITE CRAG 4½

ILL BELL 6

CAUDALE MOOR 4½ S

REST
DODD 2½

Threshthwaite
Mouth

Raven
Crag

HARTSOP
DODD 3

ANGLETARN PIKES 1½

cairn
Round How

Rooking Gill Head

tarns

Path to
BOREDALE HAUSE
and PATTERDALE

tarn

continued

THE VIEW

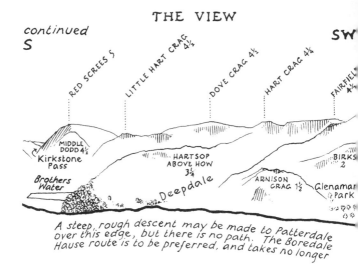

continued
S

SW

RED SCREES 5

LITTLE HART CRAG 4½

DOVE CRAG 4½

HART CRAG 4½

FAIRFIELD 4½

MIDDLE DODD 4½

Kirkstone Pass

Brothers Water

HARTSOP ABOVE HOW 3¼

BIRKS 2

ARNISON CRAG 1⅝

Deepdale

Glenamara Park

A steep, rough descent may be made to Patterdale over this edge, but there is no path. The Boredale Hause route is to be preferred, and takes no longer

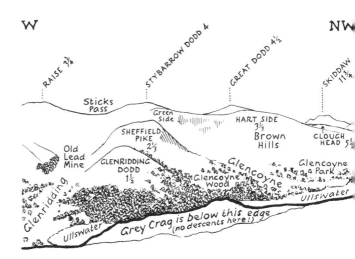

W

NW

RAISE 3¾

STYBARROW DODD 4

GREAT DODD 4½

SKIDDAW 11¾

Sticks Pass

Green side

HART SIDE 3⅓

CLOUGH HEAD 5½

SHEFFIELD PIKE 2⅔

Brown Hills

Old Lead Mine

GLENRIDDING DODD 1½

Glencoyne Wood

Glencoyne

Glencoyne Park

Glenridding

Ullswater

Ullswater

Grey Crag is below this edge (no descents here!)

THE VIEW

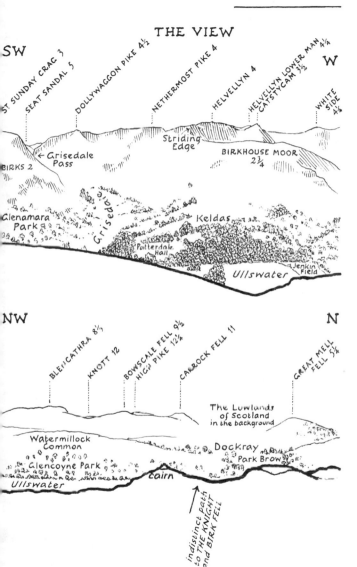

SW

St SUNDAY CRAG 3
SEAT SANDAL 5
DOLLYWAGGON PIKE 4½
NETHERMOST PIKE 4
HELVELLYN 4
HELVELLYN LOWER MAN 4¼
CATSTYCAM 3½
WHITE SIDE 4¼

W

← Grisedale Pass
Striding Edge
BIRKHOUSE MOOR 2¾

BIRKS 2

Grisedale

Clenamara Park
Keldas
Patterdale Hall
Ullswater
Jenkin Field

NW

BLENCATHRA 8½
KNOTT 12
BOWSCALE FELL 9½
HIGH PIKE 12¼
CARROCK FELL 11
GREAT MELL FELL 5¼

N

The Lowlands of Scotland in the background

Watermillock Common
Dockray
Park Brow

Glencoyne Park
Cairn

Ullswater

indistinct path to THE KNIGHT and BIRK FELL

Rampsgill Head

Spelt 'Ramsgill Head' on
old Ordnance Survey maps.

• Patterdale

HIGH RAISE
▲
Hartsop   RAMPSGILL HEAD
•   ▲ ▲ KIDSTY PIKE
                Riggindale
              ▲ HIGH STREET

MILES
0   1   2   3   4

from Gray Crag

NATURAL FEATURES

There is usually little difficulty in defining the boundaries of a mountain. If it rises in isolation there is no difficulty, and even if it is merely a high point on a ridge invariably its main slopes go down to valley-level, probably on both flanks, and the limit of its extent in other directions is, as a rule, marked by watercourses falling from the cols or depressions linking it with adjacent heights. Rampsgill Head is, geographically, a 'key' point in the High Street range, for two independent ridges of some importance leave its summit, and it is, therefore, all the more remarkable that a neat and precise definition of its natural boundaries cannot be given, largely because lower secondary summits on the side ridges are also regarded as separate fells and claim to themselves territory that would otherwise be attributed to the parent fell. It is also unusual for so prominent a height to be without an official name. Rampsgill Head is properly the name of the semicircle of high ground enclosing the rough upper reaches of the valley of Ramps Gill but is now generally attached to all the fell above and beyond, although occasionally some writers have remedied the lack of a common title by referring to the whole mass hereabouts, east of the watershed, as Kidsty Pike, but this is incorrect.

The most impressive natural feature is the fringe of crags breaking abruptly at the edge of the summit facing Ramps Gill and the long slopes of boulder debris and scree below are an indication that, before the age of decay, the rock scenery here must have been very striking. Grass predominates elsewhere but there is another steep face of rock, Twopenny Crag, falling into Riggindale. Hayeswater lies at the foot of the western slope, but the principal becks from the fell act as feeders of Ullswater and Haweswater.

Twopenny Crag

This fine arête (here seen from the
south) starts from a leaning pinnacle
on the west face and leads directly
to the top of the fell. It is littered
with loose rock and is obviously
in a state of decay; otherwise
it would surely deserve the
attention of rock-climbers

The summit crags

The eastern aspect of
the arête, here illustrated,
reveals a prominent vertical
buttress of sound, clean' rock,
not of great height but perhaps
worth carrying a rope up from Patterdale or Hartsop

MAP

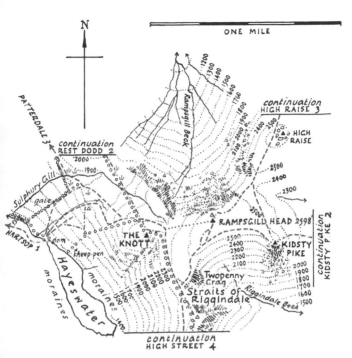

N

ONE MILE

continuation
HIGH RAISE 3

1200
1300
1400
1500
1600
1700
1800
1900
2000
2100
2200
2300

PATTERDALE 3

continuation
REST DODD 2

2000
1900

Rampsgill Beck

▲▲ HIGH
RAISE

2500
2400
2300

Sulphury Gill

gate

HARTSOP 1

dam

sheep pen

moraines

Hayeswater

moraine

▲ RAMPSGILL HEAD 2598

THE ▲
KNOTT

2500
2400
2300
2200
2100

1700
1600
1500
1400

2300
2200

Twopenny
Crag

Straits of
Riggindale

★ KIDSTY
PIKE

2000
1900
1800
1700
1600
1500

Riggindale Beck

continuation
KIDSTY PIKE 2

continuation
HIGH STREET 4

The crags above the north-west face

ASCENTS FROM PATTERDALE AND HARTSOP
2200 feet of ascent : 4½ miles from Patterdale
2050 feet of ascent : 2¾ miles from Hartsop

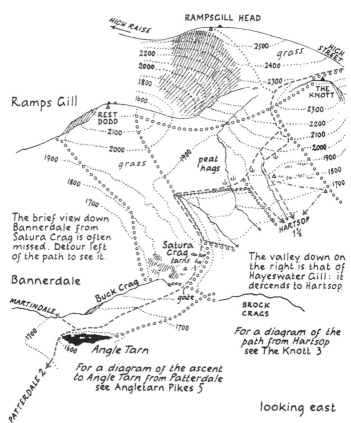

HIGH RAISE

RAMPSGILL HEAD

HIGH STREET

2500 .... grass

2400

2300

THE KNOTT

2200

2000

1800

1600

Ramps Gill

REST DODD

2100

2000

1900

1800

1700

grass

1900

peat hags

2300

2200

2100

2000

1900

1800

1700

The brief view down Bannerdale from Satura Crag is often missed. Detour left of the path to see it.

Bannerdale

Satura Crag tarns

HARTSOP 1½

The valley down on the right is that of Hayeswater Gill: it descends to Hartsop.

MARTINDALE

Buck Crag

gate

BROCK CRAGS

1700

1700

1600   Angle Tarn

For a diagram of the path from Hartsop see The Knott 3

PATTERDALE 2

For a diagram of the ascent to Angle Tarn from Patterdale see Angletarn Pikes 5

looking east

This is a most enjoyable excursion with a succession of widely differing views, all excellent ; and the route itself, never very distinct, is an interesting puzzle to unravel. In bad weather, however, there will be some difficulty, and a stranger may run into trouble on top of Rampsgill Head, where there are crags.

ASCENT FROM MARDALE
1950 feet of ascent : 3½ miles from the road end

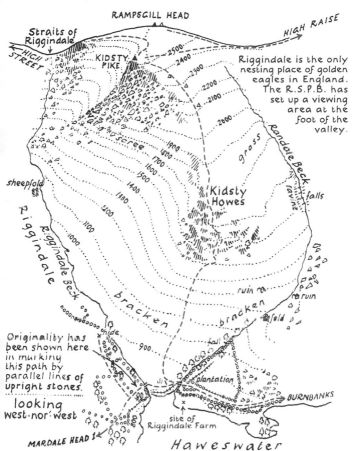

RAMPSGILL HEAD

HIGH RAISE

Straits of Riggindale

HIGH STREET

KIDSTY PIKE

2500
2400
2300
2200
2100
2000
1900
1800
1700
1600
1500
1400
1300
1200
1100
1000
900

scree

Riggindale is the only nesting place of golden eagles in England. The R.S.P.B. has set up a viewing area at the foot of the valley.

grass

Randale Beck

ravine

falls

Kidsty Howes

sheepfold

Riggindale

Riggindale Beck

bracken

bracken

ruin

ruin

fold

hide

Originality has been shown here in marking this path by parallel lines of upright stones.

looking west-nor'-west

plantation

BURNBANKS

MARDALE HEAD

site of Riggindale Farm

Haweswater

The path over Kidsty Howes replaces an old route which made use of neglected and fading paths ascending to the right of the plantation. It is a much better approach. At the top of the steep ascent the path enters an interesting world of little rocky hills.

THE SUMMIT

MARDALE ILL BELL · HIGH STREET · THORNTHWAITE CRAG

On the right sort of day, the top is a pleasant place to linger awhile. The turf is delightful, there is some outcropping rock to add interest, the rim of crags is worthy of a leisurely and detailed exploration, the views are good in all directions. A prominent, well-built cairn stands on the edge of the abrupt north-west face; thirty yards away is the highest cairn — an untidy heap of stones.

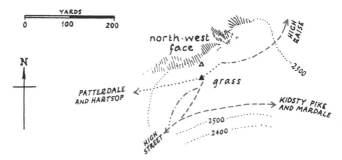

DESCENTS : For Patterdale and Hartsop, aim for The Knott to join the path there. For Mardale, use the ridge beyond Kidsty Pike, following the path over Kidsty Howes to Riggindale Beck. It should be noted that Mardale Head is uninhabited, and the only beds in the valley are at the Haweswater Hotel on the *far* side of the lake.

In mist, the edge of the escarpment is sufficiently defined to give direction: keep it on the right hand if bound for either Patterdale or Hartsop and descend easy ground to the path. For Mardale, the path will be found just to the right of the wind-shelter on Kidsty Pike.

RIDGE ROUTES

To HIGH RAISE, 2634' : ¾ mile : NE
Depression at 2450': 190 feet of ascent

Follow the edge of the crags north-east (noting the arête on the way) and join a narrow path (the old High Street) that crosses the depression and continues up the easy grass slope of High Raise opposite. When the stony top is reached leave the path and pick a way among embedded boulders to the cairn.

To THE KNOTT, 2423' : ⅓ mile · W
Depression at 2360'
65 feet of ascent

Descend the easy west slope to the wall-corner in the depression (the good path *crossed* here is the regular Patterdale to High Street route). He is tired indeed who cannot gain the summit of The Knott from the corner of the wall, and two minutes for the ascent is a generous time allowance.

To KIDSTY PIKE, 2560' : ⅓ mile · ESE
Depression at 2525': 35 feet of ascent

Kidsty Pike is unmistakable. By directly aiming for it a fair path overlooking the Riggindale face will be joined.

To HIGH STREET, 2718' : 1¼ miles : SW then S
Depression at 2340': 400 feet of ascent

Go south and join the path from Kidsty Pike, which leads down to a narrow depression in impressive surroundings. This is (or these are) the Straits of Riggindale, and from here the top of High Street may be reached simply by following the broken wall, but it is better by far to arrive there by skirting the edge of the cliffs on the left, which gives striking views.

All these routes are easy, and, with care, safe in mist

THE VIEW

Although the Helvellyn range conceals most of the western fells the view is very extensive and interesting. There is a commanding prospect of Ramps Gill from the larger cairn.

Principal Fells

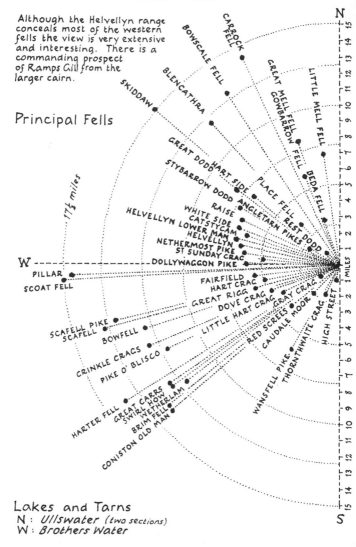

Lakes and Tarns
N : *Ullswater* (two sections)
W : *Brothers Water*

THE VIEW

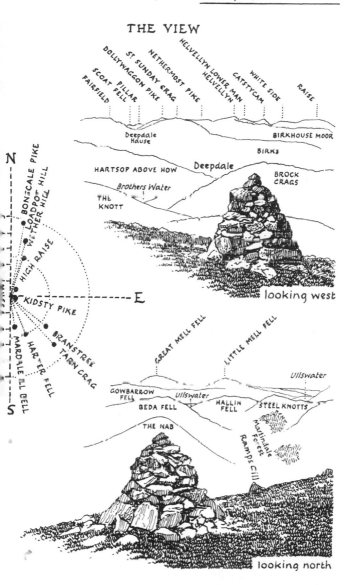

FAIRFIELD
SCOAT FELL
PILLAR
DOLLYWAGGON PIKE
ST SUNDAY CRAG
NETHERMOST PIKE
HELVELLYN
LOWER MAN
HELVELLYN
CATSTYCAM
WHITE SIDE
RAISE

Deepdale Hause

BIRKHOUSE MOOR

BIRKS

HARTSOP ABOVE HOW   Deepdale

Brothers Water

THE KNOTT

BROCK CRAGS

looking west

N

BONSCALE PIKE
WETHER HILL
LOADPOT HILL
HIGH RAISE
KIDSTY PIKE ――― E
BRANSTREE
TARN CRAG
HARTER FELL
MARDALE ILL BELL
S

GREAT MELL FELL

LITTLE MELL FELL

Ullswater

GOWBARROW FELL   Ullswater   HALLIN FELL   STEEL KNOTTS

BEDA FELL

THE NAB

Martindale Forest

Ramps Gill

looking north

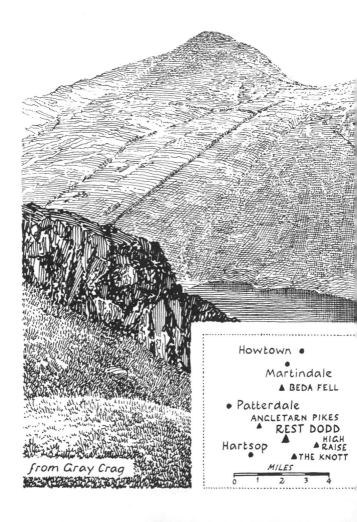

from Gray Crag

Howtown •
• Martindale
▲ BEDA FELL
• Patterdale
ANGLETARN PIKES
▲ REST DODD
Hartsop ▲ ▲ HIGH
• RAISE
▲ THE KNOTT
MILES
0 1 2 3 4

NATURAL FEATURES

The steep-sided ridge that divides Martindale into the secluded upper valleys of Bannerdale and Ramps Gill rises first to the shapely conical summit of The Nab and then more gradually to the rounded dome of Rest Dodd, which dominates both branches. It is a fell of little interest, although the east flank falls spectacularly in fans of colourful scree. Rest Dodd stands at an angle on the undulating grassy ridge coming down from the main watershed to the shores of Ullswater, and its south-west slope, which drains into Hayeswater Gill, is crossed by the track from Patterdale to High Street. Much of the fell is within the Martindale deer forest.

MAP

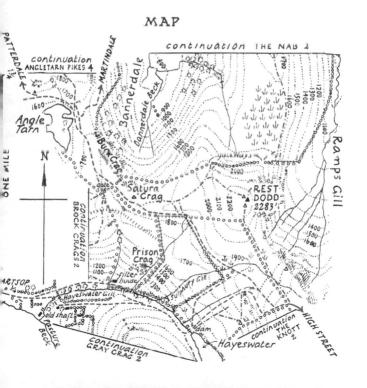

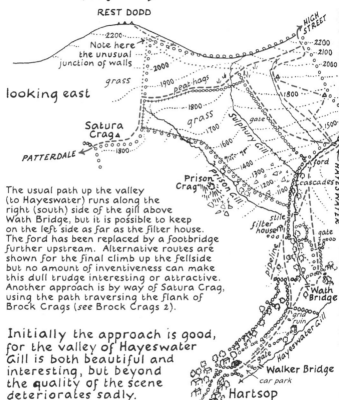

ASCENT FROM HARTSOP
1700 feet of ascent : 2 miles

REST DODD

looking east

Note here the unusual junction of walls

grass

grass

Satura Crag

PATTERDALE

Prison Crag

cascades

stile

filter house

pipeline

HIGH STREET

HAYESWATER

gate

ford

gate

Wath Bridge

grid ruin

gate

Walker Bridge

car park

Hartsop

The usual path up the valley (to Hayeswater) runs along the right (south) side of the gill above Wath Bridge, but it is possible to keep on the left side as far as the filter house. The ford has been replaced by a footbridge further upstream. Alternative routes are shown for the final climb up the fellside but no amount of inventiveness can make this dull trudge interesting or attractive. Another approach is by way of Satura Crag, using the path traversing the flank of Brock Crags (*see Brock Crags 2*).

Initially the approach is good, for the valley of Hayeswater Gill is both beautiful and interesting, but beyond the quality of the scene deteriorates sadly.

ASCENT FROM PATTERDALE
1900 feet of ascent : 3½ miles

Take the usual route to High Street (*diagrams, Angletarn Pikes 5 and High Street 5*), which traverses the slopes of Rest Dodd, but after crossing the top of Satura Crag, continue by the wall directly ahead, bearing left at the top.

(It is an interesting fact that the Patterdale-High Street route formerly followed this wall up to its top corner and down the south slope of Rest Dodd, an extra 300 feet of climbing which the present more direct path avoids. No traces remain of a path by the wall.)

THE SUMMIT

A summit-cairn with a flagpole! Such was once Rest
Dodd's distinction, but now the flagpole has gone
there is little to relieve the drabness of the
top of the fell. There are three cairns and
a natural obstacle in the shape of an
eroded peat-hag on the grassy summit.

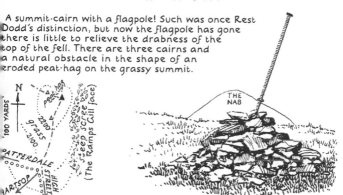

DESCENTS : Go down past the south cairn to the junction of two
broken walls. Follow the wall west to join the path from High Street
to Patterdale. Alternatively, use the path to the west.
Do not attempt any descents into Ramps Gill, which is deer forest.

Buck Crag and Heck Crag from Satura Crag

THE VIEW

The view is neither so pleasing nor so extensive as that from The Knott nearby, although the full length of the Helvellyn range is well seen. The wild and lonely head of Ramps Gill is an impressive sight. In the west, Great Gable fits snugly into the deep depression of Deepdale Hause.

Principal Fells

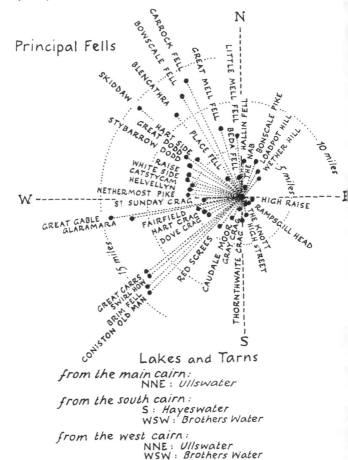

Lakes and Tarns

from the main cairn:
  NNE : *Ullswater*

from the south cairn:
  S : *Hayeswater*
  WSW : *Brothers Water*

from the west cairn:
  NNE : *Ullswater*
  WSW : *Brothers Water*
  WNW : *Angle Tarn*

RIDGE ROUTES

To ANGLETARN PIKES, 1857': 1¾ miles: W, then NW
Depression at 1600': 300 feet of ascent

An interesting walk, full of variety.

From the west cairn go down the shoulder to Satura Crag, where the path to Patterdale is joined. (*In mist, descend by the wall.*) Bear right at Angle Tarn onto the path to Beda Fell and bear left at the top of the hill. Of the many tops, the furthest is the main Pike.

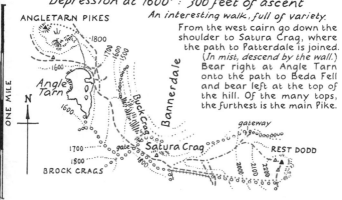

To THE KNOTT, 2423': ¾ mile: SSE
Depression at 1925': 500 feet of ascent
Merely a matter of following a wall.

From the south cairn the wall is soon reached. The depression is marshy. The High Street path is crossed at the remains of a gateway.

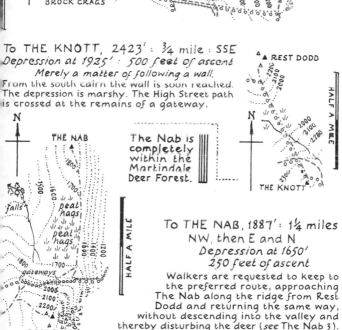

The Nab is completely within the Martindale Deer Forest.

To THE NAB, 1887': 1¼ miles
NW, then E and N
Depression at 1650'
250 feet of ascent

Walkers are requested to keep to the preferred route, approaching The Nab along the ridge from Rest Dodd and returning the same way, without descending into the valley and thereby disturbing the deer (*see The Nab 3*).

Sallows

better known locally
as Kentmere Park

1691'

from Badger Rock

▲ YOKE

SALLOWS
▲   ● Kentmere

● ▲ SOUR HOWES
Troutbeck

● Windermere

MILES

0   1   2   3   4

For most walkers, the fells
proper in this region start at
Garburn Pass and rise to the
north, but there are two hills
twins almost, immediately to
the south of the Pass, worth a
mention although these are
not strictly walkers' territory.
The higher of the two is named
Sallows (on all maps), bounding
the Pass, and has much merit
as a viewpoint and a scantier
virtue as a grouse sanctuary.
It is not worth the detour for
anyone bound for Ill Bell and
places north, and, in any case,
there is not entirely free access
to the fell and visitors may be
requested to state their business

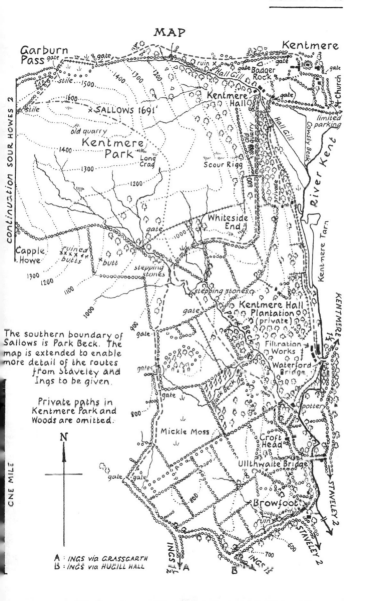

MAP

Garburn Pass

Kentmere

gate · gate · ruin · gate · Badger Rock

stile · 1500 · 1400 · 1300 · Hall Gill · Kentmere Hall · church

stile · 1600 · × SALLOWS 1691' · limited parking

old quarry · gate

Kentmere Park · 1400 · Long Crag · Scour Rigg · Hall Gill

1300 · 1200

Whiteside End · private · River Kent

Capple Howe · ruines · gate · Kentmere Tarn

1300 · 1200 · butts · butt · stepping stones

1100 · stepping stones

1000 · gate · Kentmere Hall Plantation (private)

The southern boundary of Sallows is Park Beck. The map is extended to enable more detail of the routes from Staveley and Ings to be given.

gate · Filtration Works · Waterford Bridge

Private paths in Kentmere Park and Woods are omitted.

gates · pottery

gate · Croft Head

N · Mickle Moss

800 · Ullthwaite Bridge

gate · gate · Browfoot

ONE MILE · ruin · 700 · 600

A : INGS via GRASSGARTH
B : INGS via HUGILL HALL

INGS · INGS · STAVELEY 2 · STAVELEY 2 · KENTMERE ST.

continuation SOUR HOWES 2

ASCENTS

The summit may be most easily and quickly visited from the top of Garburn Pass, where a stile in the wall gives access to the fell. Alternatively it can be gained by a mile-long ascent from the Ings-Kentmere Hall bridle-path: a simple gradient, but not easy walking.

Sallows is not, as it appears to be, a 'short cut' to Garburn Pass from the south. Apart from doubts as to trespass, its tough heather slopes compel slow progress, and time will be lost. Garburn is best reached by orthodox routes.

THE SUMMIT

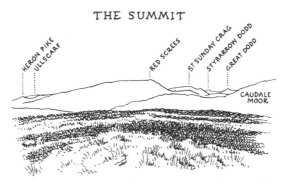

A curious curving mound of shale and grass, thirty feet long and narrow as a parapet, marks the highest part of the fell: it seems to be man-made, but is more probably a natural formation. It has no cairn. Heather and coarse grass cover the top of the fell, but there are small outcrops of rock west of the summit.

The summit mound

THE VIEW

The Lakeland scene occupies only half the panorama: it is outstandingly good to the west but unattractive northwards where Yoke fills much of the horizon. The rest of the view is exceedingly extensive, varied and interesting, covering a wide area from the Pennines across Morecambe Bay to Black Combe.

Principal Fells

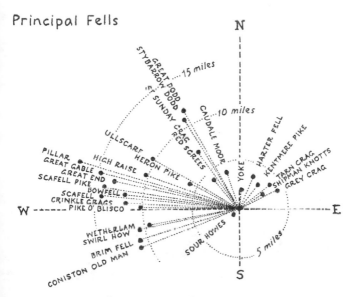

Lakes and Tarns: SSW: Windermere

Sallows from Ullthwaite Bridge

Haweswater Hotel
●

● Swindale Head

Mardale
Head ●
▲ SELSIDE PIKE

▲ BRANSTREE

▲ HARTER FELL

MILES

0   1   2   3   4

from Mosedale Beck
near the waterfalls

NATURAL FEATURES

One of the lesser-known fells is Selside Pike on the eastern fringe of the district, commanding the head of the shy and beautiful little valley of Swindale. Its neglect is scacely merited, for although the summit is a dull grass mound with little reward in views, the fell has an extremely rugged eastern face that closes the valley in dramatic fashion: here are dark crags, rarely-visited waterfalls, a curious dry tarn-bed set amongst moraines and, above it, a perfect hanging valley, the two being connected by a very formidable gully.

For countless ages Selside Pike has looked down upon Swindale and seen there a picture of unspoiled charm. Fifty years ago engineers took over the valley with the idea of building a reservoir; now they have gone, mercifully leaving the valley as they found it. The little farmstead of Swindale Head remains totally unspoiled.

Selside Pike from the Old Corpse Road

Selside Pike 3

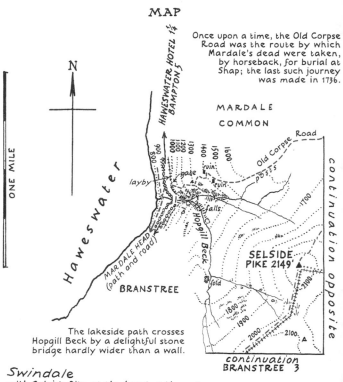

MAP

Once upon a time, the Old Corpse Road was the route by which Mardale's dead were taken, by horseback, for burial at Shap; the last such journey was made in 1736.

ONE MILE

Haweswater

HAWESWATER HOTEL 1¼
BAMPTON 5

MARDALE COMMON

Old Corpse Road

POSTS

ruin
gate
ruin
layby
falls

Hopgill Beck

MARDALE HEAD (path and road)

BRANSTREE

SELSIDE PIKE 2149'

continuation opposite

fold

The lakeside path crosses Hopgill Beck by a delightful stone bridge hardly wider than a wall.

continuation BRANSTREE 3

Swindale
with *Selside Pike at the head of the valley*

MAP

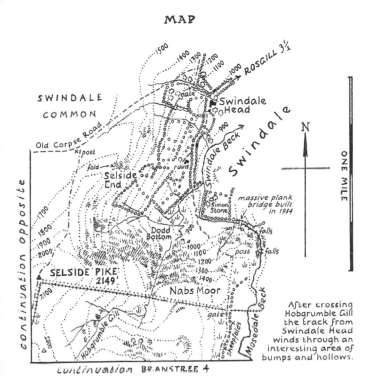

SWINDALE COMMON

Old Corpse Road

x post

fold

Selside End

ruins

Dodd Bottom

Swindale Beck

Swindale

1500
1400
1300
1200
1100
1000

ROSGILL 3½

gate

Swindale Head

900

N

ONE MILE

Simons Stone

massive plank bridge built in 1984

falls

post   falls

1700
1800
1900
2000

continuation opposite

2100

▲ SELSIDE PIKE 2149'

Nabs Moor

1000
1100
1200
1300
1400
1500

2000

Hobgrumble Gill

gate

Mosedale Beck

Sheepfolds

continuation BRANSTREE 4

After crossing Hobgrumble Gill the track from Swindale Head winds through an interesting area of bumps and hollows.

Swindale Head

ASCENT FROM SWINDALE HEAD
1200 feet of ascent : 1½ miles (via the north-east ridge)
1350 feet of ascent : 2¼ miles (via the Mosedale path)

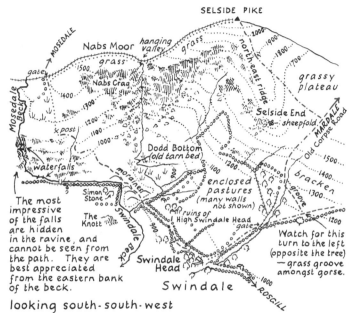

SELSIDE PIKE

looking south-south-west

The most impressive of the falls are hidden in the ravine, and cannot be seen from the path. They are best appreciated from the eastern bank of the beck.

The quality of the scenery deteriorates when the tedious higher slopes are reached. If returning to Swindale, ascend by the ridge and descend by the wire fence, making a detour to see the waterfalls.

THE SUMMIT

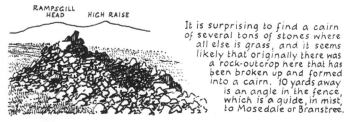

It is surprising to find a cairn of several tons of stones where all else is grass, and it seems likely that originally there was a rock-outcrop here that has been broken up and formed into a cairn. 10 yards away is an angle in the fence, which is a guide, in mist, to Mosedale or Branstree.

THE VIEW

The view towards Lakeland is disappointing, being confined to the surroundings of Mardale except for a glimpse of distant fells over the Straits of Riggindale.
Eastwards, however, there is a splendid prospect of the Pennines, with Shap village prominent.

Principal Fells

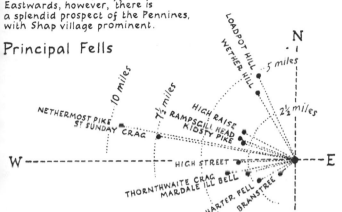

Lakes and Tarns

NNW: *Haweswater*
Small Water and *Blea Water* can both be seen by walking 30 yards W in the direction of High Street.

RIDGE ROUTE

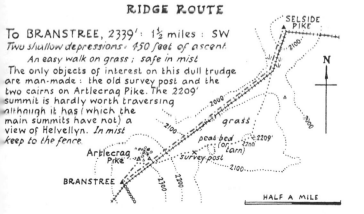

To BRANSTREE, 2339′: 1½ miles : SW
Two shallow depressions: 450 feet of ascent.
An easy walk on grass ; safe in mist
The only objects of interest on this dull trudge are man-made : the old survey post and the two cairns on Artlecrag Pike. The 2209′ summit is hardly worth traversing although it has (which the main summits have not) a view of Helvellyn. *In mist keep to the fence.*

HALF A MILE

Shipman Knotts

from Stockdale

▲ HARTER FELL

▲ KENTMERE   ▲ TARN
    PIKE   CRAG

▲
ILL BELL   ▲ GREY
        ▲   CRAG

SHIPMAN KNOTTS

• Kentmere

Longsleddale •

0   1   2   3   4

Shipman Knotts is of moderate altitude and would have called for no more than the brief comment that it is a shoulder of Kentmere Pike had it not earned for itself a separate chapter by reason of the characteristic roughnesses of its surface. Rocky outcrops are everywhere on the steep slopes, persisting even in the woods of Sadgill, although these seldom attain the magnitude of crags. This fell is usually climbed on the way to Harter Fell from the south and its rock should be welcomed for there is precious little beyond. The south slope carries the path from Kentmere to Longsleddale

MAP

continuation KENTMERE PIKE 4

Goat Scar
River Sprint
quarry road
fold
stile
gully
Dun Crag
Rough Crags
Withered Howe
gap
gap and h.post
SHIPMAN KNOTTS 1926
bridge
gap
Sadgill
Overend
Hallow Bank
Pout Howe
GATESGARTH
Brock-stones
Wray Crag
old quarries
gutter
signpost
Stile End
River Kent
parking place
gate
gate
footbridge
gate
cairn indicates summit of pass
Low Bridge
Kentmere
Green Quarter
→ STAVELEY 3¾

The cart-track linking Stile End and Sadgill
is the regular highway between Kentmere
and Longsleddale. Highest point: 1120 feet.

ONE MILE

ASCENTS

from Kentmere : 1400 feet of ascent : 2¼ miles
from Sadgill : 1300 feet of ascent : 1½ miles

Shipman Knotts is usually climbed as a means of
gaining access to the Harter Fell ridge, but is an
interesting short expedition in itself. The ascent
is most easily made alongside the wall running up
from the summit of the Stile End-Sadgill 'pass'; but
from Kentmere the ridge north of the fell-top may
be reached by a grooved path leaving Hallow Bank.
Safe in mist if the wall route is followed.

*The summit
from the south*

THE SUMMIT

KENTMERE PIKE

Three rocky knolls, on
the east side of the wall
form the summit, and of
these the middle one is
highest. It is without a
cairn.
DESCENTS: Cross the
wall and follow it south
to the pass, where turn
left for Longsleddale,
right for Kentmere. In
mist, this is a safe route

*The summit-ridge
from Goat Scar*

THE VIEW

The northern half of the panorama is restricted to nearby heights of greater elevation; the southern is open, extensive and pleasing. There is a good view of Longsleddale.

Principal Fells

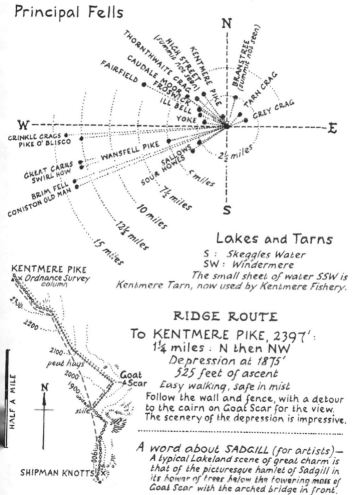

Lakes and Tarns

S : Skeggles Water
SW : Windermere
The small sheet of water SSW is Kentmere Tarn, now used by Kentmere Fishery.

RIDGE ROUTE

To KENTMERE PIKE, 2397':
1¼ miles : N then NW
Depression at 1875'
525 feet of ascent
Easy walking, safe in mist
Follow the wall and fence, with a detour to the cairn on Goat Scar for the view.
The scenery of the depression is impressive.

- -

A word about SADGILL (for artists) —
A typical Lakeland scene of great charm is that of the picturesque hamlet of Sadgill in its bower of trees below the towering mass of Goat Scar with the arched bridge in front.

Sour Howes

1585'

better known locally as
Applethwaite Common

from Troutbeck

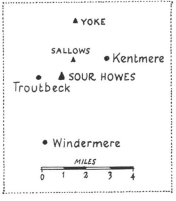

```
              ▲ YOKE

        SALLOWS
           ▲        ● Kentmere
      ●       ▲ SOUR HOWES
  Troutbeck


          ● Windermere
              MILES
      0   1   2   3   4
```

Although all maps agree that
the summit of this fell is named
Sour Howes, its broadest flank,
carrying the Garburn Pass Road
down to Troutbeck, is far better
known as Applethwaite Common;
this flank is traversed also by
the pleasant Dubbs Road. There
is little about the fell to attract
walkers, and nothing to justify
a detour from the main Ill Bell
ridge to the north, for although
the views are really good they
are better from the main ridge.
There is heather on the eastern
slopes, and therefore, inevitably,
grouse; and therefore, inevitably,
shooting butts : one may admire
the construction of these butts
but be glad they are now disused.

MAP

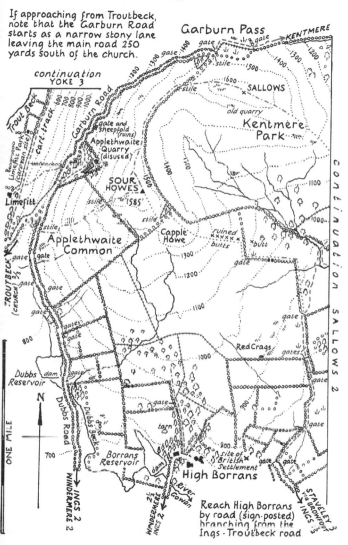

If approaching from Troutbeck, note that the Garburn Road starts as a narrow stony lane leaving the main road 250 yards south of the church.

continuation YOKE 3

Garburn Pass

KENTMERE

SALLOWS

Kentmere Park

old quarry

Garburn Road

gate and sheepfold (ruins)

Applethwaite Quarry (disused)

SOUR HOWES 1585'

Capple Howe

ruined butts

butt

continuation SALLOWS 2

Trout Beck

cart-track

Limefitt Park (caravan site)

Limefitt

Applethwaite Common

TROUTBECK (CHURCH) 2/3

Red Crags

gates

Dubbs Reservoir

N

ONE MILE

Dubbs Road

Dubbs Beck

Borrans Reservoir

tarn

dam

site of British Settlement

High Borrans

River Gowan

WINDERMERE via INGS 2

INGS 2

STAVELEY via BROWFOOT INGS

Reach High Borrans by road (sign-posted) branching from the Ings-Troutbeck road

ASCENTS

Sour Howes is a fell with no obvious appeal to walkers, and few other than conscientious guide-book writers will visit its summit; nevertheless it makes a pleasant walk from Windermere, Ings or Staveley, especially on a clear day for the views are good.

Two lanes leave Ings (one *via* Grassgarth and one *via* Hugill Hall) and another leaves Browfoot (two miles up the Kentmere valley from Staveley): these join, and at the terminus the old bridle path to Kentmere Hall may be followed for a mile, when it may be forsaken and a way made to the top by the shooting butts. The stile on Capple How is decrepit and unlikely to last long.

The summit is easily visited from the top of Garburn Pass, but by far the best way up is by the path from the west, which is well provided with stiles. If the two routes are combined, the latter should be left for the descent, so that the wonderful view of Windermere is kept ahead.

THE SUMMIT

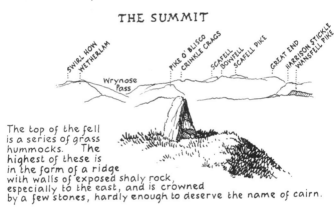

The top of the fell is a series of grass hummocks. The highest of these is in the form of a ridge with walls of exposed shaly rock, especially to the east, and is crowned by a few stones, hardly enough to deserve the name of cairn.

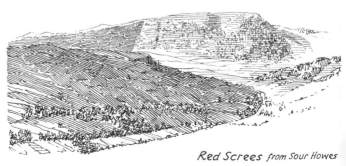

Red Screes from Sour Howes

THE VIEW

The crowded skyline in the west arrests the attention, with the vertical profile of Scafell above Mickledore prominent in the scene. Langdale Pikes are well seen between and below Great End and Great Gable. There is a very extensive and beautiful prospect southwards from the far Pennines round to Morecambe Bay and Black Combe.

Principal Fells

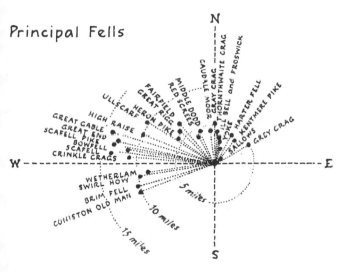

Lakes and Tarns

S: *Borrans Reservoir*
SSW: *Windermere*

Most old and disused quarries are gloomy and repellant places but Applethwaite Quarry, near the Garburn Road, is relieved from desolation by a planting of conifers and a magnificent view. A favourite with foxes, this quarry!

Applethwaite Quarry

Steel Knotts

1414'

summit named Pikeawassa

from Howegrain Beck

Wether Hill's western flank swells into a bulge, Gowk Hill, which itself sends out a crooked bony arm northwards to form a lofty independent ridge running parallel to the main range and enclosing with it the short hidden valley of Fusedale. On the crest of this ridge, rock is never far from the surface and it breaks through in several places, notably at the highest point, which is a craggy tor that would worthily embellish the summit of many a higher fell. This freakish gnarled ridge is Steel Knotts; the summit-tor is named, on the best of authority, (but not by many, one imagines) Pikeawassa *(O.S. 1" and 2½" maps)*.

Howtown
●
STEEL KNOTTS
▲   ▲ LOADPOT
       HILL
    ▲ WETHER HILL

MILES

0   1   2   3

MAP

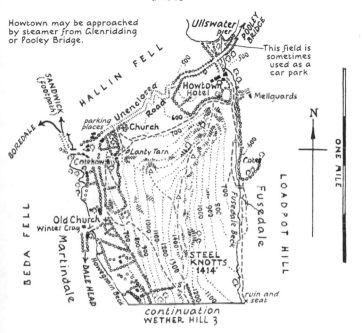

Howtown may be approached by steamer from Glenridding or Pooley Bridge.

This field is sometimes used as a car park.

ASCENTS

FROM HOWTOWN : The natural route of ascent is by the craggy ridge above Howtown. This has an intimidating aspect but it is without perils and gives an exhilarating scramble. Leave the path at its base by a concrete post above an iron plate inscribed: PWW AV and climb upwards between the rocks ; initially there is a track obscured by bracken. A cairn surmounts the steepest part of the ridge and the walking is then easy to the top of the fell.

FROM LANTY TARN : A pronounced shoulder, with two tiers of crag, descends north-west to Lanty Tarn and offers a less satisfactory route. From the tarn (a shallow pond) climb to the right (south) of the crags to a cairn above them. An easy slope then follows.

FROM MARTINDALE OLD CHURCH : This is the easiest way. Climb the fellside by the church to a good path slanting upwards (this is the Martindale path to the High Street range). Leave the path at a wall and turn up left to the ridge and again left to the top.

Although Steel Knotts is of small extent and modest elevation, it should not be climbed in mist. If caught by mist on the top, descend south to the wall and return by the path to Martindale Old Church.

THE SUMMIT

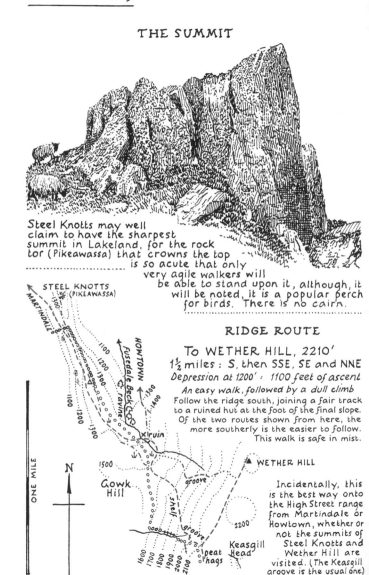

Steel Knotts may well claim to have the sharpest summit in Lakeland, for the rock tor (Pikeawassa) that crowns the top is so acute that only very agile walkers will be able to stand upon it, although, it will be noted, it is a popular perch for birds. There is no cairn.

RIDGE ROUTE

TO WETHER HILL, 2210'
1½ miles : S, then SSE, SE and NNE
Depression at 1200' : 1100 feet of ascent

An easy walk, followed by a dull climb
Follow the ridge south, joining a fair track to a ruined hut at the foot of the final slope. Of the two routes shown from here, the more southerly is the easier to follow. This walk is safe in mist.

Incidentally, this is the best way onto the High Street range from Martindale or Howtown, whether or not the summits of Steel Knotts and Wether Hill are visited. (The Keasgill groove is the usual one.)

THE VIEW

Principal Fells

This is the best viewpoint for the upper Martindale district, the highlight of a charming scene being the confluence of the remote Ramps Gill and Bannerdale valleys

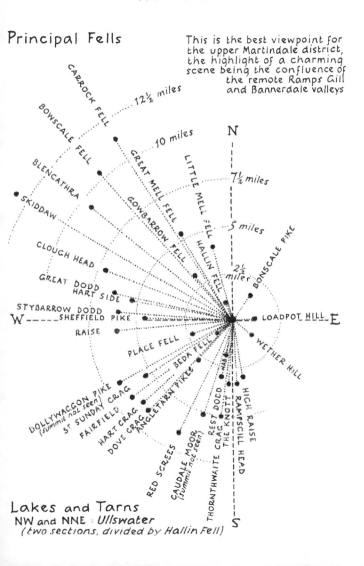

Lakes and Tarns
NW and NNE : *Ullswater*
(two sections, divided by Hallin Fell)

Tarn Crag

from Sadgill Wood

Shap •

• Swindale Head

Mardale
Head •
▲ BRANSTREE
▲ HARTER FELL
▲ TARN CRAG
KENTMERE
PIKE
▲ GREY CRAG
• Wet
Sleddale
• road
summit

Longsleddale

MILES
0   1   2   3   4   5

NATURAL FEATURES

The gradually rising wall of fells bounding Longsleddale on the east reaches its greatest elevation, and its terminus, in Tarn Crag. To the valley this fell presents a bold front, with Buckbarrow Crag a conspicuous object, but on other sides it is uninteresting, especially eastwards where easy slopes merge into the desolate plateaux of Shap Fells. It is enclosed on the north by the wide, shallow depression of Mosedale, a natural pass linking Longsleddale with Swindale in wild and lonely surroundings: here a former shepherd's cottage merely accentuates the utter dreariness of the scene. (Yet on rare occasions of soft evening light even Mosedale can look inexpressibly beautiful!) The walker hereabouts will be in no doubt, without reference to his map, that he has passed outside the verge of Lakeland.

1 : The summit
2 : Ridge continuing to Grey Crag
3 : Ridge continuing to Branstree
4 : Buckbarrow Crag   5 : Galeforth Brow
6 : Brunt Tongue   7 : Greycrag Tarn
8 : Galeforth Gill   9 : River Sprint
10 : Little Mosedale Beck   13 : Mosedale
11 : Mosedale Beck   12 : Longsleddale

looking north-east

The head of Longsleddale

MAP

Mosedale Cottage has been maintained
by the Mountain Bothy Association
since 1999. Its primitive facilities
are available, free of charge,
to anyone able to reach
this desolate spot.

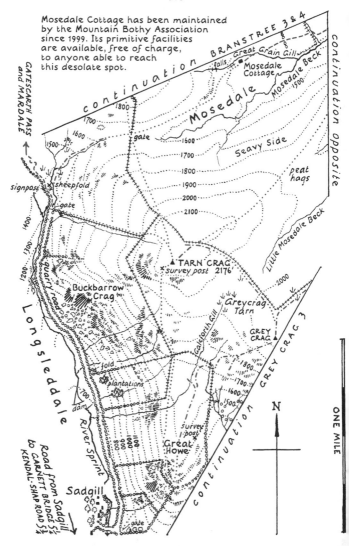

ONE MILE

MAP

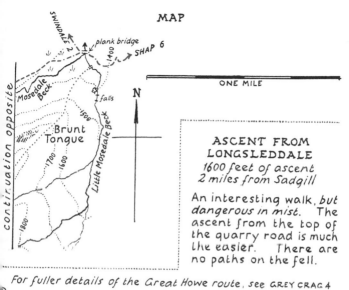

SWINDALE 2

plank bridge

1400 SHAP 6

Mosedale Beck

falls

N

1500

continuation opposite

Brunt Tongue

1700

1600

1800

Little Mosedale Beck

ONE MILE

ASCENT FROM LONGSLEDDALE
1600 feet of ascent
2 miles from Sadgill

An interesting walk, *but dangerous in mist.* The ascent from the top of the quarry road is much the easier. There are no paths on the fell.

For fuller details of the Great Howe route, see GREY CRAG 4

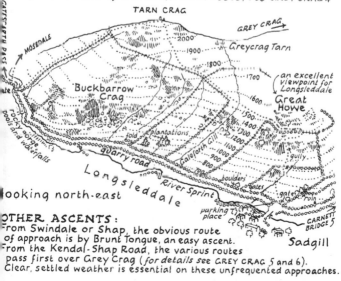

TARN CRAG

GREY CRAG

2000

1900

Greycrag Tarn

MOSEDALE

1800

1700

an excellent viewpoint for Longsleddale

GATESCARTH PASS

Buckbarrow Crag

1600

Great Howe

1500

1400

1300

rocky gorge pools and waterfalls

fold

plantations

1200

1100

quarry road

Galeforth Gill

1000

900

800

gully

boulders

gates

Longsleddale

River Sprint

gate

ruin

looking north-east

parking place

CARNETT BRIDGE 5

Sadgill

OTHER ASCENTS :
From Swindale or Shap, the obvious route of approach is by Brunt Tongue, an easy ascent.
From the Kendal-Shap Road, the various routes pass first over Grey Crag (*for details see GREY CRAG 5 and 6*).
Clear, settled weather is essential on these unfrequented approaches.

THE SUMMIT

Not until Manchester Corporation's engineers climbed Tarn Crag, in the course of their duty, and departed from it for the last time, did its summit acquire distinction: the wide dreary top then found itself left with a curious structure — a high wooden platform with a core of stone and concrete, which served for a time as a survey post during the construction of the Longsleddale tunnel conveying the Haweswater Aqueduct south. Now, eighty years later, the aqueduct is in place and the scars are gone from the valley — but the hoary survey post still stands, defying the weather and puzzling the few travellers who come this way and find no clue as to its purpose.

The highest part of the fell, marked by a small undistinguished cairn, is a hundred yards away, to the east.

DESCENTS : The routes of ascent should be used for descent.
In mist, keep strictly to the fences. Crags obstruct the direct way down into Longsleddale. Eastwards, Shap Fells are a wilderness to avoid in bad weather.

The wooden structure has now gone.

THE VIEW

Anyone who climbs Tarn Crag for a view of Lakeland will be very disappointed, for, excepting the Coniston fells, nothing is to be seen of the distant west because of the adjacent heights across the deep trench of Longsleddale. On a clear day there is ample recompense, however, in the excellent panorama from east round to south — where, for a hundred miles, the noble skyline of the Pennines and the wide seascape of Morecambe Bay present themselves to view without obstruction.

Principal Fells

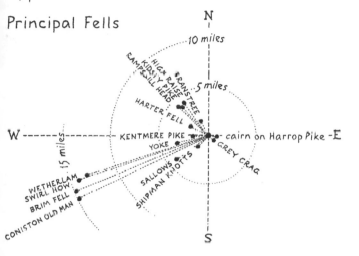

N

10 miles

HIGH STREET
KIDSTY PIKE
RAMPSGILL HEAD
RANSTREE

5 miles

HARTER FELL

W --------- 15 miles ---------- KENTMERE PIKE -- cairn on Harrop Pike -E

YOKE

GREY CRAG

SALLOWS
SHIPMAN KNOTTS

WETHERLAM
SWIRL HOW
BRIM FELL
CONISTON OLD MAN

S

Lakes and Tarns: SW: Windermere

Kentmere Pike
across Longsleddale

RIDGE ROUTES

To BRANSTREE, 2339′ : 1¾ miles : N, then NW
Depression at 1650′ : 700 feet of ascent
Rough grass, but easy gradients ; safe in mist

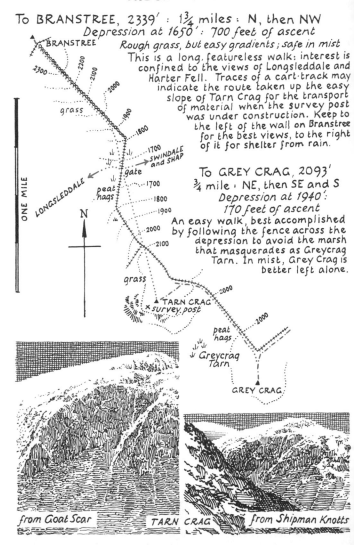

This is a long, featureless walk: interest is confined to the views of Longsleddale and Harter Fell. Traces of a cart-track may indicate the route taken up the easy slope of Tarn Crag for the transport of material when the survey post was under construction. Keep to the left of the wall on Branstree for the best views, to the right of it for shelter from rain.

To GREY CRAG, 2093′
¾ mile : NE, then SE and S
Depression at 1940′ :
170 feet of ascent
An easy walk, best accomplished by following the fence across the depression to avoid the marsh that masquerades as Greycrag Tarn. In mist, Grey Crag is better left alone.

from Goat Scar TARN CRAG *from Shipman Knotts*

Buckbarrow Crag

Thornthwaite Crag 2569'

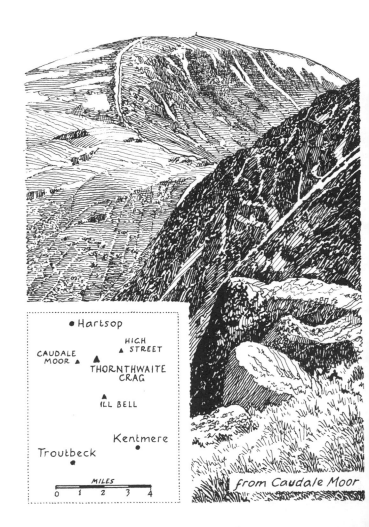

HARTSOP

HIGH STREET

CAUDALE MOOR

THORNTHWAITE CRAG

ILL BELL

Kentmere

Troutbeck

MILES
0 1 2 3 4

from Caudale Moor

NATURAL FEATURES

Occupying a commanding position overlooking four valleys, Thornthwaite Crag is one of the better-known fells east of Kirkstone, owing not a little of its fame to its tall pillar of stones, a landmark for miles around. Its name derives from the long shattered cliff facing west above the upper Troutbeck valley; there are also crags fringing the head of Hayeswater Gill and above the early meanderings of the River Kent. Apart from these roughnesses the fell is grassy, the ground to the east of the summit forming a wide plateau before rising gently to the parent height of High Street, of which Thornthwaite Crag is a subsidiary; it has, however, a ridge in its own right, this being a narrow steep sided shoulder that ends in Gray Crag, northwards. Streams flow in three directions: north to Ullswater, south to Windermere and south-east along the Kentmere valley.

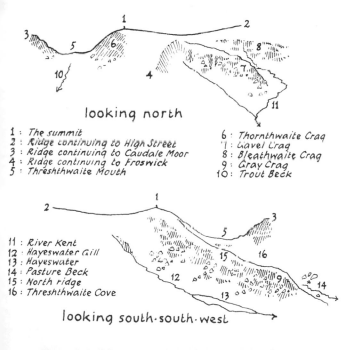

looking north

1 : The summit
2 : Ridge continuing to High Street
3 : Ridge continuing to Caudale Moor
4 : Ridge continuing to Froswick
5 : Threshthwaite Mouth

6 : Thornthwaite Crag
7 : Gavel Crag
8 : Bleathwaite Crag
9 : Gray Crag
10 : Trout Beck

11 : River Kent
12 : Hayeswater Gill
13 : Hayeswater
14 : Pasture Beck
15 : North ridge
16 : Threshthwaite Cove

looking south·south·west

Thornthwaite Crag 3

MAP

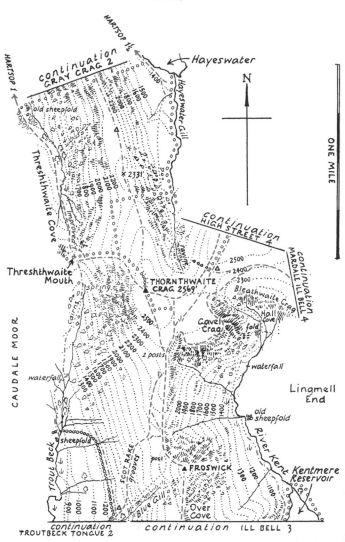

ASCENT FROM HARTSOP
2000 feet of ascent : 3¼ miles

THORNTHWAITE CRAG

HIGH STREET

CAUDALE MOOR

Threshthwaite Mouth

HIGH STREET

grass

ravine

Hayeswater Gill

GRAY CRAG

Threshthwaite Cove

grass

Pasture Beck ravine

Raven Crag

HARTSOP DODD

Hayeswater

moraines

grass

dam

sheepfold

Threshthwaite Glen

There is shelter among the boulders below Raven Crag

Pronounce 'Threshthwaite' Thresh'et

old × mine

stile
filter house

Wath Bridge

old mine

gate

ruin

gate

gate

car park

Hayeswater is a reservoir for Penrith

In mist, use the Threshthwaite route only

looking south · south · east

Hartsop

This is a very interesting and enjoyable expedition. Of the three routes illustrated, that via Hayeswater starts well but has a tame and tiring conclusion. If the return is to be made to Hartsop, Threshthwaite is the best approach, the descent being made along the north ridge over Gray Crag, which itself has an airy situation and good views.

ASCENT FROM TROUTBECK
2200 feet of ascent
5 miles via Scot Rake; 5½ via Threshthwaite Mouth

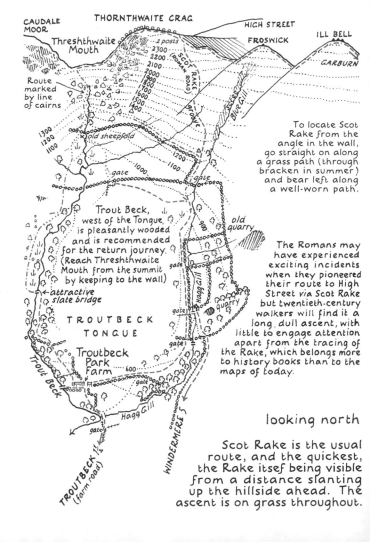

CAUDALE MOOR

THORNTHWAITE CRAG

HIGH STREET

ILL BELL

Threshthwaite Mouth

FROSWICK

GARBURN

Route marked by line of cairns

SCOT RAKE (ROMAN ROAD)

Blue Gill

2 posts
2300
2200
2100
2000
1900
1800
1700
1600
1500

groove

1300
1200
1100

old sheepfold

1000

gate

gate

1200

1100

old quarry

To locate Scot Rake from the angle in the wall, go straight on along a grass path (through bracken in summer) and bear left along a well-worn path.

Trout Beck, west of the Tongue, is pleasantly wooded and is recommended for the return journey. (Reach Threshthwaite Mouth from the summit by keeping to the wall)

900

gate

Hagg Gill

quarry

← attractive slate bridge

TROUTBECK TONGUE

gate

Troutbeck Park Farm

600

gate

The Romans may have experienced exciting incidents when they pioneered their route to High Street via Scot Rake but twentieth-century walkers will find it a long, dull ascent, with little to engage attention apart from the tracing of the Rake, which belongs more to history books than to the maps of today.

Trout Beck

Hagg Gill

gate

TROUTBECK ¼ (farm road)

WINDERMERE 5

looking north

Scot Rake is the usual route, and the quickest, the Rake itself being visible from a distance slanting up the hillside ahead. The ascent is on grass throughout.

ASCENT FROM KENTMERE RESERVOIR
1650 feet of ascent : 2 miles

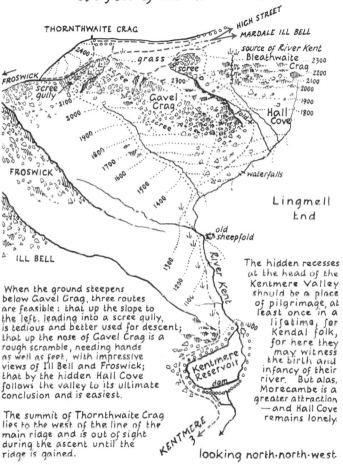

When the ground steepens below Gavel Crag, three routes are feasible: that up the slope to the left, leading into a scree gully, is tedious and better used for descent; that up the nose of Gavel Crag is a rough scramble, needing hands as well as feet, with impressive views of Ill Bell and Froswick; that by the hidden Hall Cove follows the valley to its ultimate conclusion and is easiest.

The summit of Thornthwaite Crag lies to the west of the line of the main ridge and is out of sight during the ascent until the ridge is gained.

The hidden recesses at the head of the Kentmere Valley should be a place of pilgrimage, at least once in a lifetime, for Kendal folk, for here they may witness the birth and infancy of their river. But alas, Morecambe is a greater attraction —and Hall Cove remains lonely.

looking north·north·west

This approach leads into the unfrequented dalehead of Kentmere and abounds in interest and variety all the way from the village. Rainsborrow Crag, up on the left, is a tremendous object en route, and Ill Bell and Froswick reveal themselves most effectively.

THE SUMMIT

Thornthwaite Beacon

It is sometimes difficult to recall the details of familiar summits but surely all who have climbed Thornthwaite Crag will identify it in memory by its remarkable 14-feet column, one of the most distinctive cairns in Lakeland. It stands in the angle of a wall that traverses the summit. A few outcrops of flaky rock in the vicinity relieve the general grassiness of the top of the fell.

DESCENTS: In clear weather all the routes of ascent may be reversed, but that to Kentmere via Gavel Crag is not suggested nor should routes be 'invented' as there is rough ground about. *In bad conditions*, descend to Troutbeck or Hartsop via Threshthwaite Mouth — to which the wall leads when followed north-west. For Kentmere, go to the end of the wall eastwards; here turn right along a faint path for 200 yards to a scree gully on the left, which descend.

looking north to
Ullswater

Threshthwaite Mouth

looking south to
Windermere

THE VIEW

Principal Fells

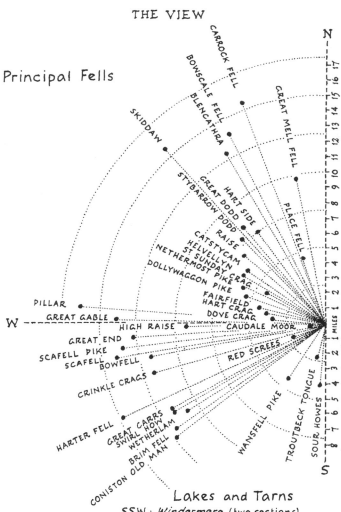

Lakes and Tarns

SSW : *Windermere* (two sections)
NNW : The upper reach of *Ullswater* may
be seen by descending the west slope for 50 yards, or by following
the wall north. N : *Hayeswater* is brought into view by a
short walk (130 yards) in the direction of High Street.

THE VIEW

The tall column, the wall, and adjacent high ground northwards between them interrupt the panorama — and various 'stations' must be visited to see all there is to see. The view is good, but not amongst the best; the northern prospect, in particular, is best surveyed from the slope going down to Threshthwaite Mouth.

The best feature in the scene is Windermere, to which the Troutbeck valley leads the eye with excellent effect.

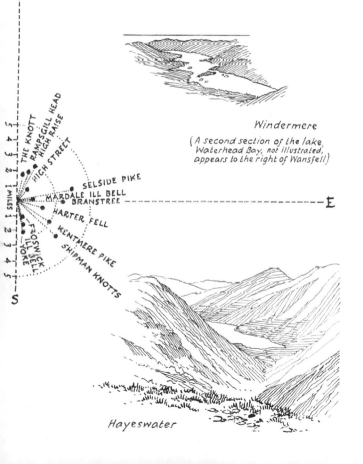

Windermere

(*A second section of the lake, Waterhead Bay, not illustrated, appears to the right of Wansfell*)

N

THE KNOTT
RAMPSGILL HEAD
HIGH RAISE
HIGH STREET

5 4 3 2 1 MILES 1 2 3 4 5

SELSIDE PIKE
MARDALE ILL BELL
BRANSTREE ------------- E
HARTER FELL
KENTMERE PIKE
FROSWICK
ILL BELL
YOKE
SHIPMAN KNOTTS

S

Hayeswater

RIDGE ROUTES

To CAUDALE MOOR, 2502': 1 mile : NW, W and WSW
Depression at 1950': 560 feet of ascent
A rough scramble, made safe in mist by walls

There is more to this walk than appears at first sight, for the gap of Threshthwaite Mouth is deep and it links slopes that are steep and rough. Keep by the wall until the broken crag of Caudale is left behind. The Caudale flank above the gap can be dangerous when the rocks are iced or under snow.

To GRAY CRAG, 2286': 1¼ miles : slightly W of N
Two minor depressions: 150 feet of ascent
An easy, interesting walk, better avoided in mist.

Straightforward walking along the descending and narrowing north ridge leads first to the nameless conical height of point 2331', then to the flat top of Gray Crag.   Two broken walls are crossed en route.   Both flanks are heavily scarped and dangerous in mist.

To FROSWICK, 2359'
1 mile
SSE then S and SE
Depression at 2100'
300 feet of ascent
A very easy walk

Follow the path by the broken wall to the south-south-east. When the wall bends left, continue straight on along the path to a junction marked by two posts. A long grassy descent leads to the final rise to the top of Froswick.

RIDGE ROUTES

To HIGH STREET, 2718': 1¼ miles : SE, then E and NE
Depression at 2475': 250 feet of ascent
A very simple walk; safe in mist

Take the prominent path east from Thornthwaite Crag and follow it as far as the wall corner. Then follow the broken wall to the top of High Street. All is grass.

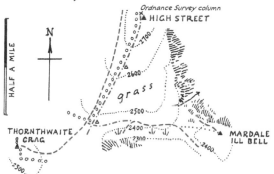

To MARDALE ILL BELL, 2496'
1⅓ miles : SE, then E, ENE and ESE
Depressions at 2475' and 2350': 200 feet of ascent
Easy walking, but a confusing area in mist

Leave the corner of the High Street wall by a plain track trending eastwards and when this curves right go straight on over long grass in the same direction, descending slightly to the depression ahead. In mist, take care not to descend to the right into Hall Cove.

Thornthwaite Crag
from the south ridge of
Caudale Moor

Troutbeck Tongue

properly named
The Tongue, Troutbeck Park

from the Kirkstone-Windermere road

▲ CAUDALE MOOR

▲ ILL BELL

TROUTBECK
▲
TONGUE

● Troutbeck

MILES

0   1   2   3

There are many Tongues in Lakeland, all of them wedges of high or rising ground between enclosing becks that join below at the tip, but none is more distinctive or aptly named than that in the middle of the Troutbeck Valley. Other Tongues usually have their roots high on a mountainside, but this one thrusts forward from the floor of the dalehead.   Although of very modest altitude, it has an attraction for the gentler pedestrian as a viewpoint for the valley, and makes an admirable short excursion in pleasant scenery from Windermere or Troutbeck or, by Skelghyll Wood, from Ambleside.

MAP

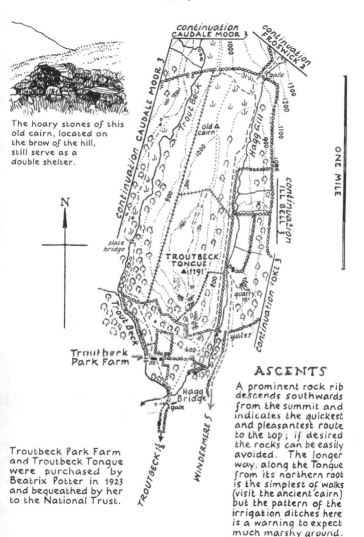

The hoary stones of this old cairn, located on the brow of the hill, still serve as a double shelter.

Map labels:
continuation CAUDALE MOOR 3
continuation FROSWICK 2
continuation CAUDALE MOOR 3
1000
gate
1300
1200
1100
Trout Beck
old cairn
Hagg Gill
1000
ONE MILE
900
continuation ILL BELL 3
N
slate bridge
TROUTBECK TONGUE △1191'
800
continuation YOKE 3
quarry
Trout Beck
gate
Troutbeck Park Farm
600
Hagg Bridge
gate
TROUTBECK 1½
WINDERMERE 5

Troutbeck Park Farm and Troutbeck Tongue were purchased by Beatrix Potter in 1923 and bequeathed by her to the National Trust.

ASCENTS

A prominent rock rib descends southwards from the summit and indicates the quickest and pleasantest route to the top; if desired the rocks can be easily avoided. The longer way, along the Tongue from its northern root is the simplest of walks (visit the ancient cairn) but the pattern of the irrigation ditches here is a warning to expect much marshy ground.

THE SUMMIT

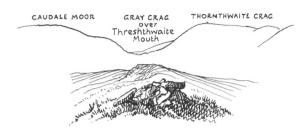

CAUDALE MOOR   GRAY CRAG over Threshthwaite Mouth   THORNTHWAITE CRAG

The rocky scramble up the south ridge from the cart-track is entertaining enough to hold out the promise of a summit equally interesting, but the promise is not fulfilled by the reality, which is a grassy knoll a little higher than several more nearby, and graced by a small heap of stones. Apart from the view down the valley to Windermere, nothing here is worth comment.

Slate bridge, Trout Beck

THE VIEW

Troutbeck Tongue is set deep in the bottom of a great bowl of hills, all of which overtop it and limit the scene. Only to the south is there an open view — of Windermere — but there is also a peep of distant fells to the west.

Principal Fells

SCAFELL PIKE

W

BOWFELL

CRINKLE CRAGS
PIKE O' BLISCO

Hart Crag (Caudale Moor)

CAUDALE MOOR

N

GRAY CRAG

THORNTHWAITE CRAG

FROSWICK

RED SCREES

ILL BELL

YOKE

5 miles

2½ miles

WANSFELL

Dodd Hill (Wansfell)

10 miles

SALLOWS

SOUR HOWES

E

S

Lakes and Tarns

SSW : *Windermere*
(middle and lower reaches)

Windermere and the Troutbeck Valley

Wansfell

1597'

CAUDALE
▲ MOOR

▲
RED SCREES

▲ WANSFELL
● Ambleside

●
Troutbeck

MILES
0   1   2   3

from High Grove

NATURAL FEATURES

Caudale Moor sends out three distinct ridges to the south, and the most westerly and longest of the three descends to a wide depression (crossed by the Kirkstone road) before rising and narrowing along an undulating spur that finally falls to the shores of Windermere. This spur is Wansfell, and, although its summit-ridge is fairly narrow and well-defined, the slopes on most sides are extensive, the fell as a whole occupying a broad tract of territory between Ambleside and the Troutbeck valley. Except northwards, the lower slopes are attractively wooded; the upper reaches are mainly grassy, but at the south-west extremity of the ridge there is a rocky bluff known as Wansfell Pike, which is commonly but incorrectly regarded as the top of the fell. Other crags masked by trees flank the Kirkstone road at Troutbeck, and Jenkins Crag in Skelghyll Wood is a very popular viewpoint. On the eastern flanks of the fell, in the village of Troutbeck, are three wells: St. John's Well, St. James' Well and Margaret's Well. Although no longer used as a source of water they can still be easily identified by their inscriptions.

MAP

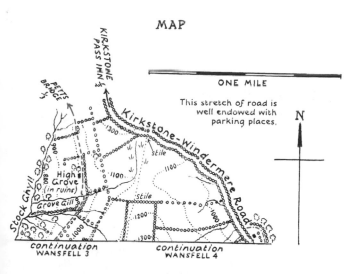

MAP

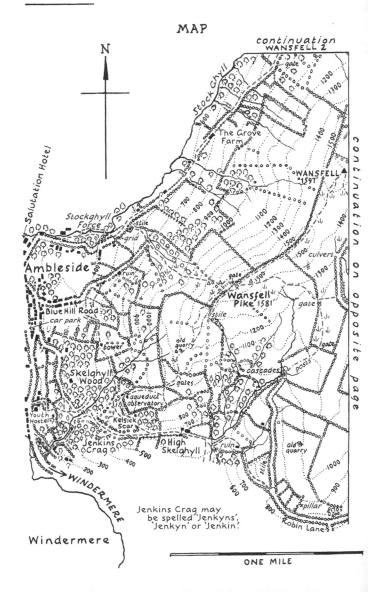

continuation WANSFELL 2

continuation on opposite page

N

Stock Ghyll

1200
1300
1400
1500

The Grove Farm

WANSFELL 1597

Salutation Hotel

Stockghyll Force

stile
grid

700
800
900
1000
1100
1200
1300
1400
1500

culvert

1300

Ambleside

ruin

gate
1500

Wansfell Pike 1581

gate

Blue Hill Road
car park

900
1000

stile

1200

1100

tower

old quarry

cascades

posts

gate

Skelghyll Wood

gates

aqueduct
observatory

800

Youth Hostel

Kelsick Scar

700

Jenkins Crag

High Skelghyll

500

ruin

old quarry

300
400

200

stile

700

600

1000

pillar

WINDERMERE

Jenkins Crag may
be spelled 'Jenkyns',
'Jenkyn' or 'Jenkin'.

800

900

Robin Lane

Windermere

ONE MILE

MAP

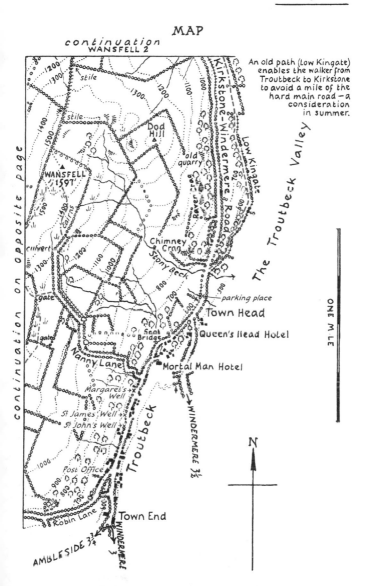

continuation WANSFELL 2

continuation on opposite page

An old path (Low Kingate) enables the walker from Troutbeck to Kirkstone to avoid a mile of the hard main road — a consideration in summer.

The Troutbeck Valley

Kirkstone-Windermere Road

Low Kingate

stile

stile

Dod Hill

old quarry

WANSFELL 1597

cairns

culvert

Chimney Crag

Stony Beck

gate

parking place

gate

Town Head

Queen's Head Hotel

Seat Bridge

Nanny Lane

Mortal Man Hotel

Margaret's Well

St James' Well

St John's Well

Troutbeck

WINDERMERE 3½

Post Office

N

Robin Lane

Town End

AMBLESIDE 3¾

WINDERMERE 3

ONE MILE

ASCENT FROM AMBLESIDE
1500 feet of ascent : 2½ miles

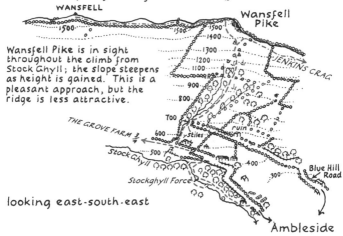

Wansfell Pike is in sight throughout the climb from Stock Ghyll; the slope steepens as height is gained. This is a pleasant approach, but the ridge is less attractive.

looking east-south-east

ASCENT FROM TROUTBECK
1100 feet of ascent : 1¾ miles

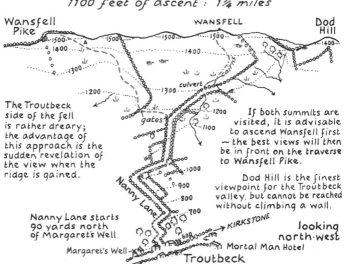

The Troutbeck side of the fell is rather dreary; the advantage of this approach is the sudden revelation of the view when the ridge is gained.

Nanny Lane starts 90 yards north of Margaret's Well.

If both summits are visited, it is advisable to ascend Wansfell first — the best views will then be in front on the traverse to Wansfell Pike.

Dod Hill is the finest viewpoint for the Troutbeck valley, but cannot be reached without climbing a wall.

looking north-west

THE SUMMIT

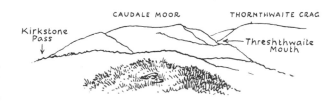

CAUDALE MOOR   THORNTHWAITE CRAG

Kirkstone
Pass

Threshthwaite
Mouth

The recognised summit of Wansfell is marked by a slender tapering cairn about four feet high, but the 2½" map shows a spot height farther north, beyond the fence and broken wall, which suggests that this is the highest point. A mile to the south-west is the lower summit of Wansfell Pike, where there is a step-stile from which paths go down to Ambleside (west) and Troutbeck (east).

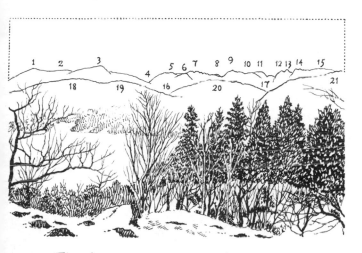

The view westwards from Jenkins Crag

1 : Coniston Old Man	8 : Scafell	15 : Pavey Ark
2 : Brim Fell	9 : Bowfell	16 : Little Langdale
3 : Wetherlam	10 : Esk Pike	17 : Great Langdale
4 : Wrynose Pass	11 : Great End	18 : Black Fell
5 : Cold Pike	12 : Loft Crag	19 : Park Fell
6 : Pike o' Blisco	13 : Pike o' Stickle	20 : Lingmoor Fell
7 : Crinkle Crags	14 : Harrison Stickle	21 : Loughrigg Fell

THE VIEW
FROM THE SUMMIT OF WANSFELL

As a viewpoint, the highest part of the summit is inferior to the lower Wansfell Pike, and, curiously, fewer fells can be seen. Nevertheless, the prospect westwards is very charming.

Principal Fells

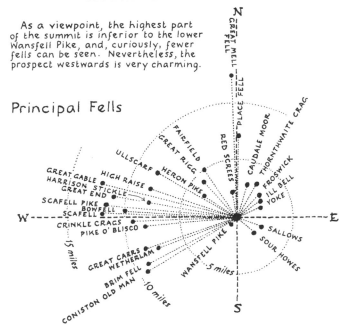

N

GREAT MELL FELL

PLACE FELL

FAIRFIELD
GREAT RIGG
RED SCREES
CAUDALE MOOR
THORNTHWAITE CRAG

ULLSCARF
HERON PIKE
FROSWICK
ILL BELL

GREAT GABLE
HIGH RAISE
HARRISON STICKLE
GREAT END
YOKE

SCAFELL PIKE
BOWFELL
SCAFELL

W ——————————————————— E

CRINKLE CRAGS
PIKE O' BLISCO
SALLOWS

15 miles

SOUR HOWES

GREAT CARRS
WETHERLAM
WANSFELL PIKE
5 miles

BRIM FELL
10 miles

CONISTON OLD MAN

S

Lakes and Tarns

S : *Windermere*
WSW : *Little Langdale Tarn*
W : *Grasmere*
W : *Rydal Water*

Red Screes, from the summit

THE VIEW
FROM WANSFELL PIKE

Wansfell Pike excels in its view of Windermere, the graceful curve of the lake showing to great advantage. Westwards, the scene is especially beautiful.
Red Screes is a fine object in the north; the east is dull.

Principal Fells

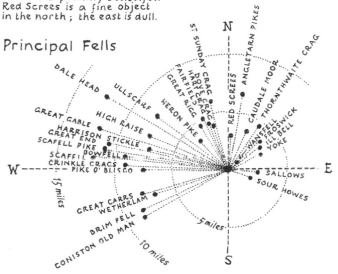

N

ST SUNDAY CRAG
DOLLYWAGGON
HART CRAG
FAIRFIELD
GREAT RIGG
RED SCREES
ANGLETARN PIKES
CAUDALE MOOR
THORNTHWAITE CRAG

DALE HEAD
ULLSCARF
HERON PIKE
WANSFELL
FROSWICK
ILL BELL
YOKE

GREAT GABLE
HIGH RAISE
HARRISON STICKLE
GREAT END
SCAFELL PIKE
BOWFELL
SCAFELL
CRINKLE CRAGS
PIKE O' BLISCO

W
E

SALLOWS
SOUR HOWES

15 miles

GREAT CARRS
WETHERLAM
BRIM FELL
CONISTON OLD MAN

5 miles

10 miles

S

Lakes and Tarns

S : *Windermere*
SW : *Blelham Tarn*
W : *Little Langdale Tarn*
WNW : *Grasmere*
WNW : *Rydal Water*
The two sheets of water on the lower slopes of Sour Howes, southeast, are reservoirs.

Windermere, from Wansfell Pike

RIDGE ROUTE

To CAUDALE MOOR, 2502'
4½ miles: N, then NE and E
Depression at 1100'
1550 feet of ascent

A long, easy, uninteresting trudge.

In May 2005, when the Countryside and Rights of Way Act came into effect, this route benefited from the removal of PRIVATE notices and the provision of stiles between Wansfell and the main road. At the time of writing, however, there is still no stile at 1700'. On grass all the way. Safe in mist, but marshy patches may then prove unpleasant.

CAUDALE MOOR

Mark Atkinson's Monument ×

2400
2300
2200
2100
2000
1900
1800

St. Raven's Edge

KIRKSTONE PASS INN

N

continuation alongside

1200
gate
stile
1100

Grove Gill

stile

1100

stile

1200
1700

stile

1400
1300

WINDERMERE 6

KIRKSTONE PASS INN

1800
1700
1600
1500
1400
1300
1200
gate
1200
stile

continuation alongside

WINDERMERE 6

WANSFELL

Aqueduct Observatory above Kelsick Scar

There are two such edifices, and a tower, above the line of the Thirlmere aqueduct along the southern slopes of Wansfell Pike.

Locating them is a pleasant way of spending a halfday: an art lies in doing this *sans* wallscaling.

ONE MILE

Stockghyll Force

Wether Hill

2210'
approx

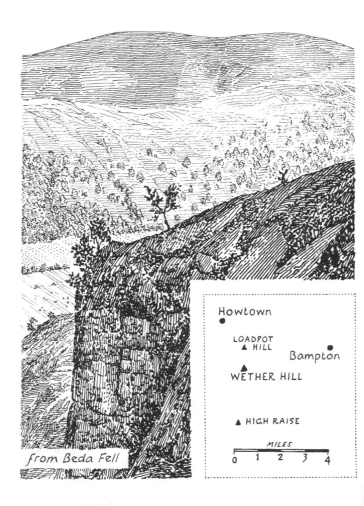

from Beda Fell

Howtown

LOADPOT
▲ HILL

Bampton

▲
WETHER HILL

▲ HIGH RAISE

MILES

0   1   2   3   4

NATURAL FEATURES

The High Street range has largely lost its appeal to the walker by the time he reaches the twin grassy mounds of Wether Hill on the long tramp along its spine northwards, and there is nothing here to call for a halt. The top, scarcely higher than the general level of the ridge, is quite without interest, while the eastern slopes are little better although traversed by two good routes from Bampton; but the western flank, characteristically steeper, has the peculiarity of Gowk Hill, a subsidiary height which itself develops into a parallel ridge running north: this encloses, with the main ridge, the little hidden valley of Fusedale. The best features of Wether Hill, paradoxically, are found in its valleys: eastwards, Cawdale Beck and Measand Beck have attractions rarely visited except by the lone shepherd; westwards, Fusedale Beck is fed from two wooded ravines, and here too is lovely Martindale.

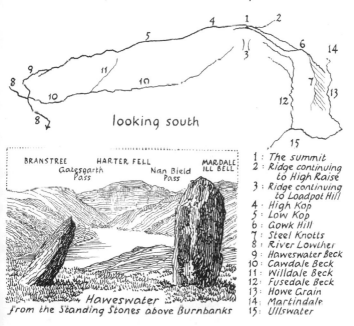

looking south

Haweswater
from the Standing Stones above Burnbanks

1 : The summit
2 : Ridge continuing to High Raise
3 : Ridge continuing to Loadpot Hill
4 : High Kop
5 : Low Kop
6 : Gowk Hill
7 : Steel Knotts
8 : River Lowther
9 : Haweswater Beck
10 : Cawdale Beck
11 : Willdale Beck
12 : Fusedale Beck
13 : Howe Grain
14 : Martindale
15 : Ullswater

MAP

Wether Hill's slopes sprawl extensively eastwards, descending gradually in easy ridges to a wide belt of cultivated land west of the Bampton - Burnbanks road — from which the ascent will generally be commenced on this side. No details of this cultivated area are depicted on the following maps (on pages 5 and 6) other than those necessary to get the walker to the open fell as quickly as possible.

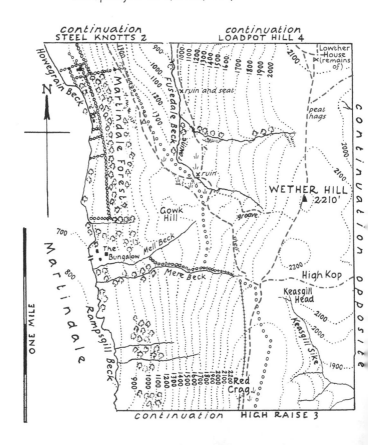

MAP

The eastern slopes of Wether Hill are bounded on the north by Cawdale Beck and on the south by Measand Beck, but some detail of the adjacent fells is, in addition, given below because they carry routes that lead onto Wether Hill.

N

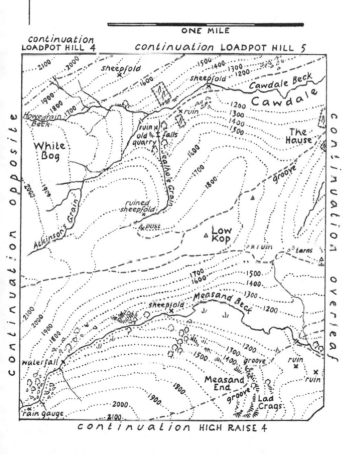

ONE MILE

continuation LOADPOT HILL 4

continuation LOADPOT HILL 5

continuation opposite

continuation overleaf

continuation HIGH RAISE 4

MAP

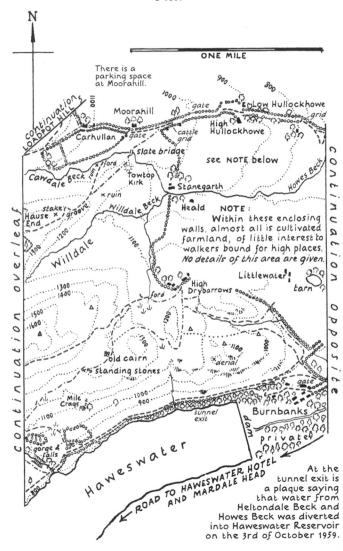

N

ONE MILE

There is a parking space at Moorahill.

continuation LOADPOT HILL

Moorahill

Carhullan

gate

cattle grid

Low Hullockhowe

grid

High Hullockhowe

see NOTE below

slate bridge

Cawdale Beck

run

ford

Towtop Kirk

Stanegarth

Howes Beck

staker

groove

x ruin

Willdale Beck

Heald

Hause End

continuation overleaf

Willdale

NOTE:
Within these enclosing walls, almost all is cultivated farmland, of little interest to walkers bound for high places. No details of this area are given.

ford

High Drybarrows

Littlewater

tarn

old cairn

standing stones

aerial

continuation opposite

Mile Craqs

tunnel exit

dam

Burnbanks

private

gorge & falls

Haweswater

ROAD TO HAWESWATER HOTEL AND MARDALE HEAD

At the tunnel exit is a plaque saying that water from Heltondale Beck and Howes Beck was diverted into Haweswater Reservoir on the 3rd of October 1959.

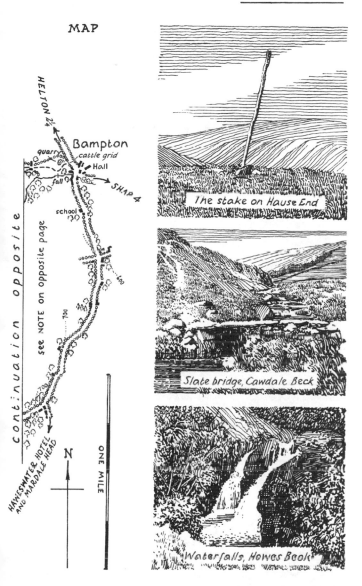

MAP

HELTON 2¼

quarry

Bampton
cattle grid
Hall

fall

SHAP 4

school

continuation opposite

see note on opposite page

700

700

HAWESWATER HOTEL
AND MARDALE HEAD

N

ONE MILE

The stake on Hause End

Slate bridge, Cawdale Beck

Waterfalls, Howes Beck

ASCENTS FROM HOWTOWN AND MARTINDALE
1750 feet of ascent, 3 miles, from Howtown
1550 feet of ascent, 2½ miles, from Martindale old church

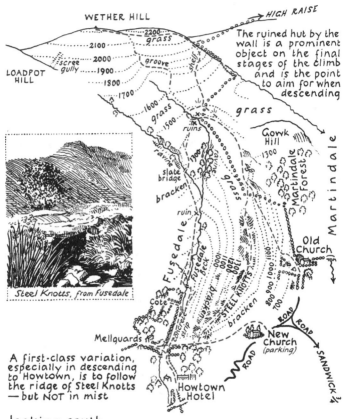

WETHER HILL — HIGH RAISE

LOADPOT HILL

2200 grass
2100
2000
1900
1800
1700
1600 grass
1500
ruins
scree gully
groove
shelf

The ruined hut by the wall is a prominent object on the final stages of the climb and is the point to aim for when descending

grass

Gowk Hill
1300
Martindale Forest

ravine
slate bridge
bracken
ruin

Fusedale
Fusedale Beck
bracken
STEEL KNOTTS
grass

Old Church

Martindale

800 900 1000 1100
700

Cote
concrete strip

Mellguards

New Church (parking)

ROAD
ROAD
ROAD

SANDWICK ¾

Howtown Hotel

Steel Knotts, from Fusedale

A first-class variation, especially in descending to Howtown, is to follow the ridge of Steel Knotts — but NOT in mist

looking south

There are many fells more worthy of climbing than Wether Hill, the final slope being very dull, but there are no more delightful starting-points than Howtown and Martindale, the approach from the latter being especially good — until the last slope is reached.

ASCENTS FROM BURNBANKS AND BAMPTON
1550 feet of ascent from Burnbanks; 1750 from Bampton.
4½ miles from Burnbanks direct, 5 via Measand Beck;
5 miles from Bampton

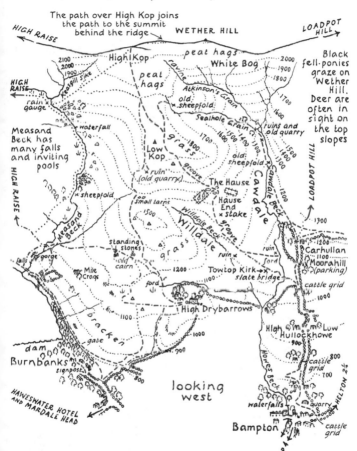

The path over High Kop joins the path to the summit behind the ridge

HIGH RAISE ←   WETHER HILL   LOADPOT HILL →

Black fell-ponies graze on Wether Hill. Deer are often in sight on the top slopes

Measand Beck has many falls and inviting pools

looking west

HAWESWATER HOTEL AND MARDALE HEAD

The Bampton route *via* Hause End is easy and interesting; the Burnbanks route across the open common is a little confusing in its early stages; on a hot day the Measand route, although pathless, is attractive.

THE SUMMIT

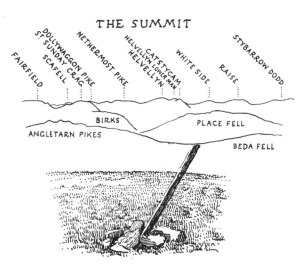

FAIRFIELD · ST SUNDAY CRAG · DOLLYWAGGON PIKE · SCAFELL · NETHERMOST PIKE · HELVELLYN LOWER MAN · HELVELLYN · CATSTYCAM · WHITE SIDE · RAISE · STYBARROW DODD

BIRKS · PLACE FELL

ANGLETARN PIKES

BEDA FELL

Two rounded grassy mounds of similar altitude, separated by a slight depression, form the summit. The more extensive of the two mounds, the southern, is quite featureless: the smaller northern mound, which is the recognised top, carries a small summit cairn in which the wooden stake shown in the illustration was formerly set; today the cairn remains but the stake has gone. The summit is popular with grazing animals of various species, but humans will find it a dreary and uninteresting place. The High Street crosses the top, but along here it is barely noticeable, being no more distinct than a sheep trod.

DESCENTS: All slopes are easy, and it is a waste of time to look for the few paths. For Bampton, pass over High Kop to join one of two good grooves. For Martindale and Howtown descend west to the ruin by the prominent broken crosswall below: leave the ruin on the *right*, passing through the gateway in the wall, for Martindale; but for Fusedale and Howtown leave the ruin well to the *left*.

In mist, there is little danger of accident, but keep out of stream-beds which run in ravines.

Former boundary stone on High Kop, with High Raise in the background

THE VIEW

Principal Fells

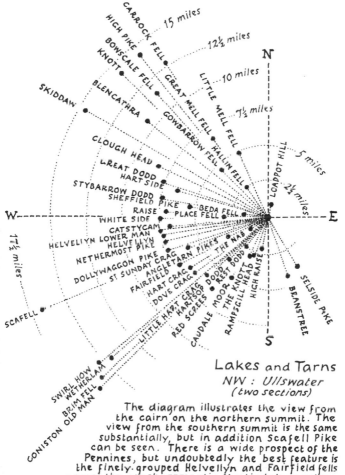

Lakes and Tarns
NW : Ullswater
(two sections)

The diagram illustrates the view from the cairn on the northern summit. The view from the southern summit is the same substantially, but in addition Scafell Pike can be seen. There is a wide prospect of the Pennines, but undoubtedly the best feature is the finely-grouped Helvellyn and Fairfield fells across the rough, romantic Martindale country.

RIDGE ROUTES

To LOADPOT HILL, 2201' : 1 mile : N
Depression at 2025' : 180 feet of ascent
An easy walk, safe in mist

Keep to the path on the left of the depression; all traces of the old path on the right side (the High Street) have vanished. The chimney stack of Lowther House, once a prominent landmark on this route, is now just a pile of stones—the summit (quartz cairn) is directly beyond.

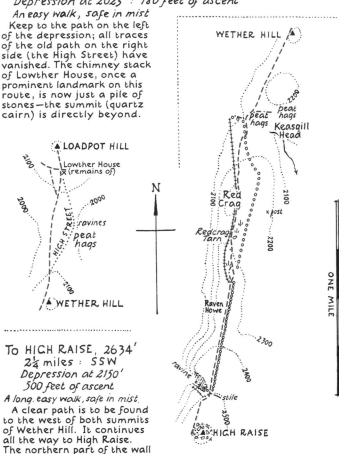

To HIGH RAISE, 2634'
2¼ miles : SSW
Depression at 2150'
500 feet of ascent
A long, easy walk, safe in mist

A clear path is to be found to the west of both summits of Wether Hill. It continues all the way to High Raise. The northern part of the wall is ruinous as far as Red Crag, its function having been taken over by the nearby fence. The southern part of the wall has been restored. When the wall ends, the path climbs across the open fell. The cairn is a hundred yards away to the left of the path at its highest point.

Measand Beck The Forces of Measand Beck, near its outlet into Haweswater, need no introduction to frequenters of this area, but the waterfalls illustrated, two miles upstream, are rarely seen.

Yoke
2316'

▲ HIGH STREET

▲ ILL BELL
▲ YOKE

Kentmere
●

● Troutbeck

MILES
0 1 2 3 4

from the Kirkstone-Windermere road

NATURAL FEATURES

Yoke is best known as the southern outpost of the Ill Bell ridge leading up to High Street from Garburn Pass, and is usually dismissed as a dull unattractive mound. As seen from Troutbeck, this seems a quite accurate assessment, but the Kentmere flank is very different, abounding in interest. On this side, below the summit, is the formidable thousand-foot precipice of Rainsborrow Crag (the safety of which is a subject of disagreement between rock-climbers and foxes) and, rising above Kentmere village, is a knobbly spur that looks like the knuckles of a clenched fist—a place of rocky excrescences, craggy tors and tumbled boulders, and a fine playground for the mountaineering novice. Both flanks of Yoke carry the scars of old quarrying operations.

grass

bracken

1 : The summit
2 : Garburn Pass
3 : Rainsborrow Crag
4 : Skeel Crags
5 : Buck Crag
6 : Castle Crag
7 : Piked Howes
8 : Ewe Crags
9 : Cowsty Knotts
10 : Raven Crag
11 : Badger Rock
12 : Lowther Brow
13 : Kentmere Reservoir
14 : Bryant's Gill
15 : River Kent
16 : Hall Gill
17 : Trout Beck

looking north

Yoke 3

MAP

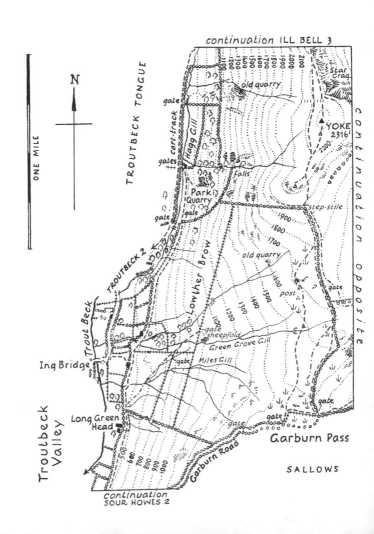

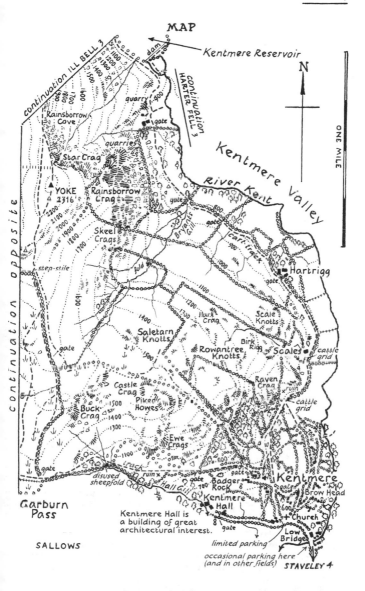

MAP

continuation ILL BELL 3

Rainsborrow Cove

Star Crag

▲ YOKE 2316

Rainsborrow Crag

quarry

quarries

gate

Kentmere Reservoir

dam

continuation HARTER FELL 3

N

ONE MILE

Kentmere Valley

River Kent

Skeel Crags

step-stile

gate

gate

Bryant's Gill

fold

cart track

gate

800

gate

Hartrigg

Scale Knotts

Saletarn Knotts

Hart Crag

Rowantree Knotts

Birk Rigg

Scales

cattle grid

Castle Crag

Buck Crag

Piked Howes

Ewe Crags

Raven Crag

ruin

cattle grid

track

disused sheepfold

ruin x

gate

Hall Gill

Badger Rock

gate

Kentmere Hall

gate

Kentmere

Brow Head

Church

Low Bridge

Garburn Pass

Kentmere Hall is a building of great architectural interest.

limited parking

occasional parking here (and in other fields)

SALLOWS

continuation opposite

STAVELEY 4

ASCENT FROM GARBURN PASS
850 feet of ascent : 1¼ miles

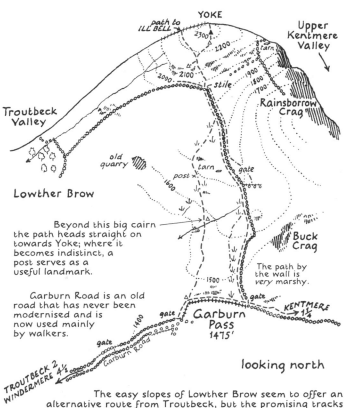

YOKE

path to
ILL BELL

2300'

2200

2100

2090 2100

Upper
Kentmere
Valley

tarn

1900
1800
1700

stile

Rainsborrow
Crag

Troutbeck
Valley

old
quarry

tarn

gate

Lowther Brow

post ×

1600

Beyond this big cairn
the path heads straight on
towards Yoke; where it
becomes indistinct, a
post serves as a
useful landmark.

Buck
Crag

The path by
the wall is
very marshy.

1500

Garburn Road is an old
road that has never been
modernised and is
now used mainly
by walkers.

gate

gate

gate

gate

Garburn Road

Garburn
Pass
1475'

KENTMERE
1¼

looking north

TROUTBECK 2
WINDERMERE 4½

1400

The easy slopes of Lowther Brow seem to offer an
alternative route from Troutbeck, but the promising tracks
climbing through the bracken from the path behind Long Green
Head (see map) do not continue far and the ascent becomes tiresome.
The route depicted here, from Garburn Pass, is better in every way.

This is a dull, easy walk, but the dreary foreground
is relieved by the splendid views to the west. There
are patches of marshy ground to the 1800' contour —
the route throughout is on grass.

ASCENT FROM KENTMERE
1800 feet of ascent : 2½ miles (3 miles via Garburn Pass)

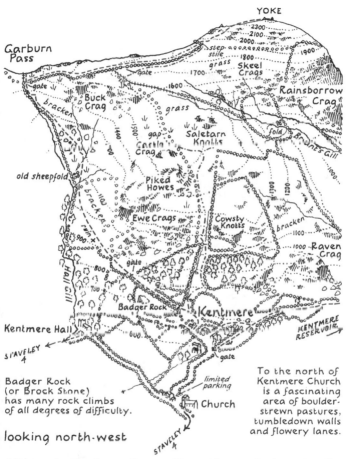

YOKE

2200
2100
2000
step-
stile
grass
1800
1900
Skeel
Crags

Garburn
Pass

gate
1700

gate
1600

bracken

Buck
Crag

grass
1500
1400

gap
Castle
Crag

Saletarn
Knotts

Rainsborrow
Crag

fold
Brock's Gill

old sheepfold

bracken

1300
1200

Piked
Howes

rain X
900

Ewe Crags

Cowsty
Knotts

1300

Raven
Crag
1000

bracken
1100

gate
1100
1000

800

Hall Gill

700

gate

Badger Rock

Kentmere

Kentmere Hall

600

KENTMERE
RESERVOIR

STAVELEY
4

gate

Badger Rock
(or Brock Stone)
has many rock climbs
of all degrees of difficulty.

limited
parking

Church

To the north of
Kentmere Church
is a fascinating
area of boulder-
strewn pastures,
tumbledown walls
and flowery lanes.

looking north-west

STAVELEY
4

Although Garburn Pass offers the easiest route, the
craggy screen rising steeply behind the village will
tempt the more adventurous walker : the top of the
spur is a maze worth exploring, but only the route
depicted guarantees to avoid unclimbable walls.

THE SUMMIT

ILL BELL

HIGH STREET

MARDALE ILL BELL

The highest point on the broad grassy top is a small rock-sided platform with a cairn. Another cairn (a better viewpoint) stands 130 yards to the south. The wire fence illustrated has gone.

DESCENTS : A short descent down the western slope brings into view a good track skirting the summit: this, followed to the left (south), leads to the wall that goes down to Garburn Pass.

In mist. note that the north-east and east slopes are entirely dangerous, and that the lower western flank is very rough: it features, in a walled enclosure, the bracken-concealed, fearful abyss of Park Quarry, a fall into which would definitely end the day's walk. From the top cairn, descend west (110 yards only) to the track and turn left; alternatively, use the path to the south from the summit—both will lead to the wall going down to Garburn Pass. When you get to the pass, turn left for Kentmere or right for Troutbeck.

ILL BELL

ILL BELL

scree gully
Star Crag

line of posts

tarn   best view
of Kentmere
Reservoir

post

×post

grass

direction of →
RAINSBORROW CRAG

2200

best view
of Windermere

grass

GARBURN PASS

YARDS
0   100   200

Park Quarry—in the sheltered depths of which flowers bloom and ferns flourish in December

THE VIEW

This is a good viewpoint, more particularly for the wide sweep of country and sea southwards. Of the Lakeland scene, the prospect due west is especially attractive.

Principal Fells

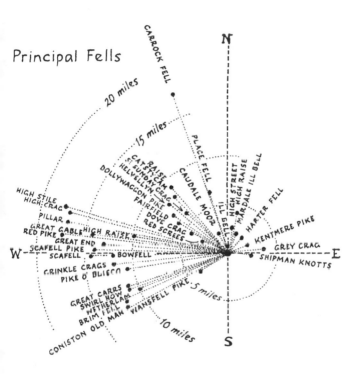

Lakes and Tarns

SSW : Windermere (much better seen from the south cairn : a very beautiful view)

SW : Blelham Tarn

To see Kentmere Reservoir, visit the edge of Star Crag, where the reservoir comes suddenly and dramatically into view north-east

RIDGE ROUTE

To ILL BELL, 2484': ⅔ mile : N
Depression at 2180': 300 feet of ascent
An easy climb, safe in mist

Pass a pair of old iron straining posts and cross the depression with the escarpment close by on the right. This is a simple walk in clear weather, but, although there is no difficulty in mist, it *may* then be not quite so easy to get safely off the top of Ill Bell.

HALF A MILE

Raven Crag

Buck Crag

Badger Rock
(Brock Stone)

West face

East face

This isolated rock stands within fifty yards of the Garburn path, just beyond the last buildings of Kentmere. A well-known local landmark, it has little fame outside the valley. Although the base of the rock is now silted up, there is little doubt that it is a boulder fallen from the fellside above, a theory supported by the cavities beneath (a refuge for foxes), and it may well be the biggest boulder in Lakeland. There are rock-climbs on it of all degrees of difficulty.

Rainsborrow Crag

THE FAR EASTERN FELLS
Some Personal Notes
in conclusion

It would be very remiss of me if I did not take this first opportunity publicly to acknowledge, with sincere gratitude, the many kind and encouraging letters that followed the publication of Book One. There have also been offers of hospitality, of transport (I have no car nor any wish for one), of company and of collaboration, and of financial help — all of which I have declined as gracefully as I could whilst feeling deeply appreciative, for I am stubbornly resolved that this must be a single-handed effort. I have set myself this task, and I am pigheaded enough to want to do it without help. So far, everything is all right. Sufficient copies of Book One were sold to pay the printer's bill, and here again I must thank all readers who recommended the book to others, for it is perfectly clear that, lacking full facilities for publicity and distribution, it could hardly have succeeded otherwise.

I have just completed the last page of Book Two, and feel like a man who has come home from a long and lonely journey. Rarely did I meet anyone on my explorations of the High Street fells. Usually I walked from morning till dusk without a sight of human beings. This is the way I like it, but what joys have been mine that other folk should share! Let me make a plea for the exhilarating hills that form the subject of this book. They should not remain neglected. To walk upon them, to tramp the ridges, to look from their tops across miles of glorious country, is constant delight. But the miles are long, and from one place of accommodation to another they are many. The Far Eastern Fells are for the strong walker and should please the solitary man of keen observation and imagination. Animal and bird life is much in evidence, and not the least of the especial charms of the area is the frequent sight of herds of ponies and deer that make these wild heights their home.

Perhaps I have been a little unkind to Manchester Corporation in referring to Mardale and Swindale in this book. If we can accept as absolutely necessary the conversion of Haweswater, then it must be conceded that Manchester have done the job as unobtrusively as possible. Mardale is still a noble valley. But man works with such clumsy hands! Gone for ever are the quiet wooded bays and shingly shores that Nature had fashioned so sweetly in the Haweswater of old; how aggressively ugly is the tidemark of the new Haweswater! A cardinal mistake has been made, from the walker's point of view, in choosing the site for the new hotel: much more convenient would have been a re-built Dun Bull at the head of the valley, or better still amongst the trees of The Rigg. For a walker who can call upon transport, however, the new road gives splendid access to the heart of the fells.

I leave this area to renew acquaintance with the more popular and frequented heights in the middle of Lakeland — the Langdale, Grasmere and Keswick triangle. This is a beautiful part of the district, and I shall enjoy it; but it is a weakness of mine to be for ever looking back, and often I shall reflect on the haunting loneliness of High Street and the supreme loveliness of Ullswater. It will please me then to think that this book may perhaps help to introduce to others the quiet delights that have been mine during the past two years.

Autumn, 1956   AW.